CAFFEINE FOR THE CREATIVE TEAM

150 EXERCISES TO INSPIRE GROUP INNOVATION

CAFFEINE FOR THE CREATIVE TEAM

150 EXERCISES TO INSPIRE GROUP INNOVATION

Stefan Mumaw & Wendy Lee Oldfield

Cincinnati, Ohio
www.howdesign.com

For more resources for designers, visit www.howdesign.com.

13 12 11 10 09   5 4 3 2 1

Distributed in Canada by Fraser Direct
100 Armstrong Avenue
Georgetown, Ontario, Canada L7G 5S4
Tel: (905) 877-4411

Distributed in the U.K. and Europe by David & Charles
Brunel House, Newton Abbot, Devon, TQ12 4PU, England
Tel: (+44) 1626-323200, Fax: (+44) 1626-323319
E-mail: postmaster@davidandcharles.co.uk

Distributed in Australia by Capricorn Link
P.O. Box 704, Windsor, NSW 2756 Australia
Tel: (02) 4577-3555

Library of Congress Cataloging-in-Publication Data

Mumaw, Stefan.
  Caffeine for the creative team : 150 exercises to inspire group innovation / Stefan
Mumaw and Wendy Lee Oldfield. -- 1st ed.
      p. cm.
  Includes bibliographical references and index.
  ISBN 978-1-60061-118-6 (pbk. : alk. paper)
  1. Commercial art--Technique. 2. Graphic arts--Technique. 3. Creative ability--Problems,
exercises, etc. 4. Creative thinking--Problems, exercises, etc. I. Oldfield, Wendy. II. Title.
  NC1000.M83 2009
  741.6068'3--dc22

                          2008051683

Edited by Amy Schell
Designed by Wendy Lee Oldfield
Art directed by Claudean Wheeler
Production coordinated by Greg Nock

Stefan Mumaw

Stefan Mumaw graduated with a BFA in graphic design from Chapman University in 1996. Since that time, he has written two books on the subject of web design (*Simple Web Sites* and *Redesigning Web Sites*) along with the creative staple *Caffeine for the Creative Mind*. He has taught design classes at Chapman University; directed the creative department at The Brainyard, a small advertising agency in Costa Mesa, California; and is currently the Director of All That Rocks at Kansas City-based creative shop Reign. Stefan has been undeservingly blessed with a beautiful wife, Niqua, and a princess in the form of a daughter, Caitlyn. He's also been undeservingly cursed with Ed, the cat.

This book is dedicated to the greatest team leader I know. She has taught me how to honor people over product, all while managing the often frantic bustle of the everyday. *To my Baby Doll, Niqua.*

Wendy Lee Oldfield

Wendy Lee Oldfield was born in South Africa, and has lived in Greece, the Netherlands and the United States. After graduating in 2004 with a BFA in graphic design from Chapman University, Wendy established her design company, Vekay Creative. In 2006, she coauthored *Caffeine for the Creative Mind* with Stefan Mumaw. *Caffeine for the Creative Team* is her second book. Wendy enjoys long walks through the Elwynn Forest, poking Mamegomas with her ninja boyfriend, and consuming mass quantities of ketchup. She resides in Southern California with a frost-spec roommate and two spicy birds.

Contents

More Contents

And Even More Contents

Surprise...More Contents

Guess What? More Contents

The End of the Contents!

"... And we want to see concepts Friday."

Friday. Like, the end of this week Friday. Four days away Friday. Just once, you say silently as your mind spins, you'd like more than half a week to generate ideas. Imagine, you think, what you and your team could come up with if you had the luxury of, oh, say, a whole week to spend. You begin asking yourself the dreaded question: How come we're continually asked to generate these brand-altering, buzz-inducing, award-winning ideas with such improbable time constraints? You can't even get through asking yourself the question before you offer the answer.

Because you succeed at it every single time.

You built your team around this exact recurring scenario. You spent weeks making sure the people you've chosen to build your business around are the right fit for your philosophy. You've turned away countless jaw-dropping portfolios in favor of the folks who had the talent and the disposition to work within the unique culture you've built. Your team is hand-selected for their ability to sit across the table from this exact client, hear these exact words and react in the same exact way.

Let's do it.

Leading this team isn't easy, but you trust them with everything. You trust them because they've proven over and over again that they are on board with your philosophy, they grasp your vision and, most importantly, they buy into the process you've developed. It's not that difficult for them to believe, really. You value the same things, you encourage big thinking and they respond by giving it to you. You learned long ago that you aren't in the business of design or advertising or marketing or PR, you're in the idea business. Your clients pay you for how you think, and as such, you spend your time in the right place: idea generation. The ideas need time to be executed, no doubt, but a bad idea perfected flawlessly is, as they say, nothing more than the proverbial polished dookieturd.

You realized long ago that putting effort and time and thought into idea generation produces the type of thinking you want to be known for. You spend real time together generating ideas. These are not mindless meetings, they are intimate occasions. You don't gather the forty people who work in your building together in the conference room, lay down the edict that they need to come up with great ideas for your client right now, and expect full participation and creative results. You take a term that has been beaten up, trashed and left for dead very seriously. It's a term that causes convulsions among staffers and trepidation among employees, and that puts the fear of boredom and office politics into the hearts of cubicle-dwellers everywhere: brainstorming.

Brainstorming has received a bad rap over the years, and rightly so. Corporate managers have misused and devalued the process of brainstorming in lieu of oatmeal-textured results. But not you. You value idea generation so much so that you've developed a process that equips your team with the best possible environment and most fertile mindset to generate the ideas that make your clients famous. And because you fully believe that idea generation is a communal act, you're willing to share your technique and offer your advice to team leaders everywhere. That's the kind of leader you are…you're a giver! And we thank you for that. Now get going, you have a presentation in four days and your team is waiting for the e-mail that tells them when they should rush the walls of Idealand for yet another epic battle. Your method and process you've left here. Good luck. We'll see you carting in the harvest on Friday.

The Right Number of Brainstormists

Conventional wisdom would say, "The more brains there are in the room, the more ideas will emerge." Unfortunately, conventional wisdom has never been locked in a room with twenty other people, the boss at the whiteboard waiting for someone to utter the perfect idea. Conventional wisdom, were he there in that room, would do what almost everyone else is doing: waiting patiently for the meeting to end. No one wants to be the one to offer a bad idea into a room of peers, superiors and that hot chick from accounting. It's much safer to sit quietly and agree with something someone else says, as long as everyone else is agreeing with it, too.

If conventional wisdom wanted to incite action and get the most out of the people in the room, he would see that brainstorming is better served as an intimate occasion. Four to seven people is a good-size group. It means everyone will have a voice, everyone can contribute and there's a broad enough range of perspectives and experiences to allow ideas to be picked up by someone else and taken to a new place. Too many people encourages hiding or, worse, devaluation. Too few people and there aren't enough diverse perspectives to transport ideas.

Don't Surround Yourself
With Other Yous

Creatives are attracted to creatives. Those who are in the business of ideas have been programmed that accountants or client services directors or office managers don't have anything valuable to offer. Human nature is to surround ourselves with like-minded people, lessening the chance of conflict. But true brainstorming invites conflict in small, productive doses. As author and creative coach Sam Harrison says, "Brainstorming should be just that: stormy."

Brainstorming sessions that contain people who have similar thought patterns and familiar perspectives are going to generate ideas that tend to be shallow and predictable. Brainstorming sessions that mix people from different perspectives and experiences, people who solve problems in completely different ways, produce ideas that have a chance to grow. Include those accountants and client services directors and office managers. You'll be surprised at how many different directions an idea can come from.

If a variety of office personalities are unavailable, consider engaging vendors and freelancers. Look at bringing in your photographer, that great local freelance illustrator, a web developer, the executive producer from the film production studio you work with. These people solve problems in a myriad of ways, and none of them are the way you solve problems. Assembling a diverse team of problem solvers heightens the chance of generating unexpected results.

No Pop Brainstorming Quizzes

Nothing is less fruitful than a surprise brainstorming session. After spending all morning spec'ing paper or stripping out chain-link fencing from its background, it's difficult to turn off the production side and turn on the instant creativity side. We're good, but we're not that good.

Give your team a few days' notice that you're going to have a brain-storming session, and tell them what you're going to be generating ideas for. By alerting your team ahead of time, you give a group of creative idea generators a couple days to think on their own. They will come to the brainstorming session with a few initial ideas in hand, giving the meeting a jump start and providing ammunition for discussion. Often, it's the hybrid of one of these ideas that starts to take flight by other people in the group applying their perspectives to the idea, which begets additional growth. Soon, you're presented with an idea that's bigger than everyone and owned by the group.

New Input, Familiar Output

Ideas are generated by mixing input with experience, meaning we take in information and combine it with our own unique experience to generate an idea. The quality and relevance of that input makes a lasting mark on the quality and relevance of the ideas produced. Providing subject-oriented input before brainstorming sessions will help produce fresh ideas during it. You can go to a museum or art gallery for inspiration, but forming input and inspiration that directly ties to the subject of the brainstorming is a powerful fire starter. If you're generating ideas for a tennis retailer, hang out at a tennis club or watch a live tennis match. If you're coming up with ideas to make a yarn store famous, go to an arts and crafts show or take a knitting class. Take the time to create subject-appropriate input before idea sessions and you'll get more targeted output.

Once you've scheduled and executed that fantastically tailored, new-environment input, take all that knowledge and all those ideas and return to a comfortable, familiar place to generate ideas. While fresh and new inspires creative thought, the comfort of a familiar place facilitates the sharing of those ideas. If you have that familiar "idea room," where everyone is accustomed to generating ideas in, go to that place for the download. If you don't have an idea room or some other familiar place you generate ideas, choose a setting that is relatively free of distractions. It may seem like a great idea to hold your tennis retailer brainstorming session outside by the courts while people play, but the distraction of the setting will detour the act and growth of output. Take those ideas back to a familiar place and share what you have.

Have Something Up Your Sleeve

As creative and inventive as your brainstorming sessions are, if you do the same thing each time, in the same order each time, with the same people each time, you're bound to get the same results each time. Ask the folks living in Hawaii where they'd vacation, and few will say, "Why would I go anywhere else when paradise is here?" When you're surrounded by the extraordinary every day, it's bound to become ordinary.

Budgets and time and circumstance certainly have influence on your ability to produce custom brainstorming sessions, but it's important to keep something unexpected. When your team knows that you have something new in store for them each time you plan a brainstorming session, they will come in with more anticipation and more passion, and be prepared to give you more for giving them more. If the goal is to produce unexpected ideas, be willing to be unexpected yourself.

If You Unroll It, They Will Draw

At Sullivan Higdon & Sink in Kansas City, Missouri, brainstorming meetings are held in rooms that have whiteboards for walls. Why? So people can record ideas as they come. So powerful was the practice, they brought the whiteboard walls outside of the conference rooms and into the work space, so people could hold impromptu brainstorming meetings and share ideas in passing, and the rest of the agency could participate, even if they were nowhere near the original thought.

While it may not be practical to line your conference room walls with whiteboards, you can take the time to get a large roll of butcher paper and cover the tables with idea canvases. Put out pens, pencils, markers, crayons, colored pencils...anything that affords people the ability to sketch and draw, note and process thought. Make it as boundless as possible, don't regulate what they draw or write, let it be an organic space that begs to be marked, and you'll find they will begin to think in the same open nature that they begin to doodle, revealing more ideas.

Bringing In The Play

Doesn't it seem that ideas always hit you when you don't expect it? Walking through an amusement park with your family, at a baseball game, hiking, running, playing. Ideas always seem to come unscheduled. Why can't you just write down in your day planner "November 5, 2 P.M.: Generate amazing ideas"? Unfortunately, ideation doesn't work that way. When our minds are open and free, we leave a lot of room to let ideation happen naturally. In the moments that we are engaged in some form of play, our minds are active and almost always in a positive frame. This makes for the perfect environment to be receptive to ideas. On November 5 at 2 P.M., we have no idea what frame of mind we will be in, but it almost certainly will be less playful than when we are engaged in play itself. So how do you combine the mind-set and fertile creative environment of play with the scheduled, time-focused world of professional creativity? You only have two choices: Schedule your brainstorming meeting while you're playing, or bring play into your brainstorming meeting.

Brainstorming should be a playful, active process. It should be light and free-flowing, and you should all laugh a lot. Think about the subject of the ideation and set up the room with purposeful toys or things that can be thrown around or thumbed through. For that tennis client, pepper the room with tennis balls, project a tennis match on the screen or roll out fake grass to simulate the playing surface. If you're ideating for that yarn store client, put different types of yarn and needles on the table, let people try to knit, play a how-to video or set up mannequins with knitted sweaters and scarves. Include snacks and drinks, even tailoring those to be focused around the theme or subject of the ideation. You want your team to want to spend time thinking with each other, so spend the time to create an environment that will encourage them to do that.

Valuing Time

One of the characteristics of a brainstorming meeting that has facilitated its reputation for being a complete waste of time corporately is the time aspect itself. "When we produce a viable solution" is a terrible marker of a meeting's duration. It puts unhealthy pressure on the meeting participants to continue to pursue lukewarm ideas in order to get out of the meeting and on to their own responsibilities.

Set a time limit for the brainstorming meetings. Folks are far more likely to buy into a brainstorming session if they know that it will indeed end at some point. Anywhere from an hour to two hours is generally enough time to get into the meat of a subject. The first part of any brainstorming meeting serves to prime the participants to generate quality ideas, and as the meeting continues, you'll find better ideas are offered as participants begin to get past the expected ideas and into the unexpected. They also have time to consider and use germs of ideas others have offered. Setting a time period from the start lets everyone know you value their time, and in return, they'll value the purpose of the meeting.

Start the Fire With a Creative Match

To start a campfire, you need kindling. To light the kindling, you need a match. Without the small, temporary light of that match, the raging campfire you'll have moments later will never come to fruition. Ideation is a lot like that. You have to start small and work to big.

Throughout our day, we bounce back and forth between ideation, execution and management. We have an idea, work on making that idea come to life and manage the time and resources that idea needs to live. Most of the time, the idea was a small percentage of that day; the rest was spent seeing that idea through.

When we are asked to participate in a brainstorming session, we are being asked to put aside all of those tasks that are forefront on our minds and focus on creative thought. That transition is difficult and often requires a primer, a buffer that tells us "turn that off and turn this on." That's what the exercises in this book are for.

The exercises in this book are meant to be matches to the kindling. They're meant to initiate a shift in focus and prime the participants to begin to think in creative, alternative ways. They are a transition from the execution and management side of our profession to the creative side. Have fun with them, keep them light and encourage buy-in with them. The more open your team is during the exercise, the quicker they will remove the masks of responsibility to think and share openly.

Leave The Judge at The Door

We hear the question all the time, "What's the quickest way for me to kill the creativity in the room and completely discourage an open, loose, creative exchange?" Our response is always the same: "Judge."

Nothing will destroy creativity thought faster than judging the value of the idea on the spot. No one wants to offer an idea that is slightly off the beaten path if there's even a remote chance the idea will be mocked and scorned as soon as it leaves their mouths. The fact is, the idea in and of itself may suck worse than any idea ever uttered, but if that idea even has a kernel of a chance that someone else can take a part of it and apply his or her perspective to it and take it in a new, viable direction, you most certainly want that idea on the table, despite its inherent suckiness.

Encourage a free flow of ideas by instructing everyone that no one will be judging the viability of the ideas during the meeting; you simply want to put as much on the table as possible so others have a chance to apply their perspectives and experiences to them. Write down the ideas on a whiteboard or chalkboard, someplace where the team can see them as they come out. That will encourage branches and offshoots that perhaps wouldn't normally grow. When the meeting is over, go back through with whomever you've entrusted with the project and judge the quality of the ideas then.

Be The Coach, Not The Owner

Coaches are natural leaders. They lead by understanding that it's not about them, it's about the team. Their job is to prepare the team to play by guiding them to their strengths and getting out of the way. They read the flow of the game, make strategic decisions to put their team in a position to succeed, then let the team take it from there. They are a guide, not a focus.

Leading a creative team is like coaching. You have to know the strengths and weaknesses of your team, position yourselves to maximize your strengths, then guide the team to places where those strengths will have the best chance at success. Brainstorming is the game, and your job is to read the flow and offer guidance. When there are gaps in the conversation, or when the team is straying down a road that might not be as fruitful, guiding them to explore other areas and encouraging alternative views puts them in the position they need to succeed. Look at the problem from a different angle, change perspectives, tell a story and recall experiences. Think of yourself as the rails to a bridge. Without the rails, they could stray too close to the edge and fall over, or, worse, they could stay in the middle out of fear of falling. With the rails in place, they're free to explore the entirety of the bridge without fear and without consequence.

Capture Residual Ideas

Ever have a verbal fight or confrontation with someone and spend the next few days mulling over what you "should" have said? We come up with all kinds of witty comebacks or perfect sentences when we've had the time to fully remove ourselves from the emotion of the moment and think objectively.

Similarly, how many times have we left a brainstorming meeting and had residual ideas hours or days later? Subconsciously, we're still ideating. We can't turn it off. Some of the best ideas we've developed have come when the emotion or direction of a brainstorming meeting has settled, and we're left with the raw thoughts and ideas presented. Those thoughts mix with experiences we failed to connect during the meeting but are very much in play now. This simmering of ideas should be encouraged and collected.

Set up an informal meeting a day or two later to discuss some of the original ideas. This could be at lunch, in a comfortable setting or just around the workplace. Don't have a formal list of the ideas that came from the meeting, as this isn't necessarily a brainstorming meeting, it's a collection meeting. See what ideas the team remembers from the brainstorming meeting. Those will often be the strongest directions, as they're the most memorable internally. The purpose of the gathering is to see if anyone has thought of any residual ideas. Doing this informally alleviates the natural desire to insert purpose into a "meeting" by contributing something meaningful. There very well could be nothing offered up as residual thought, but knowing that you would be gathering informally, participants may be more apt to capture those residual thoughts as they occur.

Put On the Back-Patter Hat

In every team environment, there are personalities that reveal themselves. Aggressive participants often will grab hold of the conversation while shy, passive participants will be less apt to openly engage the team. Both are valuable to the process and both are needed to find success. Each person contributes a perspective that is uniquely his or her own, and it's the careful mixture of these personalities and perspectives that makes for an active, thriving brainstorming session.

Even the most creative participant struggles with ideation from time to time. We're human. There are times when the ideas simply aren't flowing like they usually do. In those times, the other members of the team pick up the slack. That's why the communal team approach is so successful: diversity of personality, perspective and community.

You want to nurture this dynamic by meeting with participants face-to-face and encouraging them for the job they did. Nothing will resonate louder with team members than if you pass them in the hall the day after a brainstorming session and offer a "Hey, great job yesterday; your thoughts were fantastic" or "Hey, great job yesterday; don't be afraid to speak up and throw your ideas out there; you have great perspective and I need you to share that." This positive reinforcement will encourage future participation and promote complete buy-in for further brainstorming sessions.

2

PERSON EXERCISE

Get Out of My Way, I'm Drawing Horns!

Stefan Bucher's Daily Monster (www.dailymonster.com) is a great example of the concept of "creativity of the moment," the thought that we can grow creatively in large ways by exercising creative thoughts in small, digestible opportunities. Today, each of you is going to use a "pencil" (check the wiki entry if you don't know what a "pencil" is) to create a monster. The only restrictions are: (1) once you put the pencil down to start drawing, you can't lift it back up—scribble, scratch, shade, do whatever you want, but you can't remove the pencil from the paper until you're done—and (2) you and a partner are working together to create one monster, so you must both start at the same time on the same piece of paper working on the same monster. You can talk it out as you go, or stay silent and read from one another's direction what you can add to the monster. Make sure you have enough space around a table to move, get different perspectives and see what's been created.

14

4

PERSON
EXERCISE

Follow the Rules, Just Not Those Rules

We have a world full of rules, like it or not. As designers, we spend many long hours learning all the rules—layout rules, color rules, contract rules. Then, we spend the rest of our lives learning how to break the rules, but doing it ... by the rules. With so many rules and so many years learning how to get around the rules, we're certain to make a few rules on our own.

That's your task today: Come up with five rules for being a designer (or insert your profession of choice), according to your experience. When you have your five rules, come together with a partner and combine your rules. If you have rules that seem similar, combine them to be one rule and brainstorm a replacement. In the end, you should have the ten rules for being a designer—according to you, the rule-makers of the land!

A Turkey Carcass Is a Terrible Thing to Waste

3
PERSON EXERCISE

Leftovers. Frankly, I'm not a "leftover" guy, but Thanksgiving leftovers have become a staple of post-Thanksgiving lunch bags nationwide. Many people debate the perfect result of holiday leftovers, from the traditional turkey sandwiches to turkey casserole to turkey fondue, prepared with a mix of leftover turkey, sweet potatoes and a heavy dose of cheddar cheese. (Ugh, thank you, Rachael Ray.) But there is still something left on the table that doesn't get talked about. There is a "leftover" of almost every Thanksgiving meal that is unused, discarded and overlooked.

The turkey carcass.

Mmmm...carcass. The leftover part of the turkey once all the turkey meat has been stripped for sandwiches and fondue. What of that? Are we to give this old friend so much attention during the preparation part and then cast it aside as if it means nothing? I say to thee, nay! The task for you and at least two other carcass-repurposers today is to come up with a use for the abandoned turkey carcass. One of you should be the starter, and describe, draw, photo-manipulate or, if you're feeling especially motivated, actually use and photograph a new purpose for a real turkey carcass. When you have started the textual, visual or actual thread, send or give it to the next person in the group to further the purpose. Send it along to the third group member to finish the repurposing and complete the project. You are guaranteed to remember the exercise at Thanksgiving and perhaps be tempted to follow through when dinner's over!

Minty Fresh Garlicky Breath

As I was brushing my teeth this morning, I was observing something I've never really looked at closely: the toothpaste tube. A strange creature, this tube...a rich combination of marketing messages and chemical explanations intended to convince me to use said paste on a regular basis, promising me a more enriched lifestyle if I do. But marketing messages can only be effective if the message is tailored for the individual. I began thinking. What if "cool mint" and "whitening power" weren't enough to sway me to put down my trusty Aquafresh and try something new? What if they convinced me that using this toothpaste would be as satisfying as a corn dog from the fair? Or freshly popped popcorn with butter and salt? Now that would be a powerful message...for me. What about you?

Your exercise today is to create the ultimate toothpaste ... but for your partner. Pair up, and take hat you know about your partner and create the perfect toothpaste for him or her. Either find a tube online and design one, or simply write out a description of the toothpaste and what it offers. If you get yours back and it simply says "fresh reath," you might want to invest in a pack of mints.

Is That a Swing or a Rocket Pod?

Kids are pretty technologically savvy these days. In today's culture, with movies, video games, iPods and computers, kids are getting farther and farther removed from the laygrounds of our youth. As kids get older and technology provides new avenues of playful diversion, jungle gyms and swings seem so antiquated.

Until now.

Get three other participants for your exercise today. Your task is to create the ideal children's playground for today's youth. You can do this one of two ways: either each of you create your own "play apparatus" and combine the four items into one playground, or collaborate to design the entirety of the playground together. Consider technology, weather, durability, safety, longevity and, most of all, fun. Either draw the objects and playground, or if you're more of a wordsmith than a designer, create a story or part of a story that describes how children would interact with the objects in your team's playground.

Plaid Tastes Like Brown and Purple Mixed Together, Huh?

In the movie *Martian Child*, an orphan (played by Bobby Coleman), who thinks he's from Mars, pulls off a couple of cool stunts (like changing the lights for parental figure John Cusack as he drives) in the name of Martian intuition. One of the kid's most outrageous claims (and subsequent proofs) was that he could taste color. John Cusack's character made the boy close his eyes while he fed him various colored M&M's, inviting the boy to reveal what color the candy was each time. The boy called each one correct. As magical as that feat may be, it begs the question:

What does color taste like?

That's your exercise today. You and a partner have to describe the taste of the following colors, but they can't taste like a fruit (that's too easy!):

Red Blue Green Purple Yellow

Orange Brown Black White

And, just for fun, add plaid to the list.

Split up the colors between you and your partner, and define in words or pictures what each color tastes like.

Marc Kimball Price (N.Sycu..)

3
PERSON EXERCISE

Don't Call Clients Wankers Until You're Sure They've Left

Rules are everywhere. They define our society and ensure everyone lives in harmony. Without rules, anarchy would reign. It's for another discussion whether that would be good or bad, but for this discussion, we're going to focus on rules that are meant to bring positive results.

Most rules are a list of things *not* to do. In essence, you can boil most rules down to starting with the word "don't." That's your exercise for today.

Get two other participants and start an e-mail or blog thread revolving around creating the rules for something. It can be the rules of your environment, the rules of dealing with clients, the rules of dating, the rules of owning a dog…whatever you'd like. The only restriction is that they all start with the word "don't."

Start by offering the first rule and sending it to the next person in the group. That person adds to the list and continues to send it along, each person adding to the rules. Choose to end the session however you like, whether that's a set number or a set time frame, or you can keep it going indefinitely.

If your name is Henry and you get back the rules and one of them is "Don't hang around Henry," quit immediately.

Twisted Christmas

This exercise can be done anytime throughout the year, but it will be far more fun when Christmas is in sight. Desktop backgrounds are removable, temporary canvases that can serve to become great creative inspiration, or just twisted executions of a demented mind. We prefer dementia. We think you do, too.

Get three other participants for today's diversion. You will be creating desktop backgrounds for someone else in the group. Either randomly choose your partner like a perverse holiday gift exchange, or choose round-robin style. You are to create a desktop background combining one element from each of the following lists:

4

PERSON EXERCISE

List 1

Twelve drummers drumming
Eleven pipers piping
Ten lords a-leaping
Nine ladies dancing
Eight maids a-milking
Seven swans a-swimming
Six geese a-laying
Five gold rings
Four calling birds
Three French hens
Two turtle doves
A partridge in a pear tree

List 2

A butter knife
A police mug shot
A worm
A surgical tool
A celebrity
A typical office object
An insect or rodent repellant

When complete, send your twisted Christmas gift to the person you chose and listen for the scream of acceptance!

The Staring Ball World Championships Is Starting

There is a small window of time each year that is hallowed among sports fans. It's the month of October, where you get baseball, football, basketball *and* hockey, all at the same time. What an amazing time of the year for professional sports!

But while our favorite major sports are woven into the fabric of our culture, our favorite minor sports, the fringe games and athletic activities that get little airtime and even fewer participants, are often overlooked. When's the last time you had to choose between the Lakers–Suns game or that chainsaw-throwing competition on "The Ocho"? Our fringe sports need something to move them to the forefront of our attention. They need to piggyback on the success and popularity of our major sports. What they really need is to be *combined* with our major sports.

Your task today is to combine/mix/weave a major sport with a fringe sport or activity. First, you and a partner need to write one major sport and one fringe, scarcely known—or even made-up—sport on a piece of paper. (You can decide who gets to come up with what sport.) Once you have your major/minor sport combination, you must brainstorm to define how the two sports are combined to make one sport, with bits of both activities, rules, consequences and competition. After you have defined your new sport, describe the worst injury ever reported during the play of your new sport.

Stop! Do Not Enter! Moose Crossing!

Street signs are a ubiquitous part of our daily transportative lives. (Is "transportative" a word? I digress...) With so many streets and so much guidance to be provided, we need street signs to keep us from driving our cars off cliffs or into each other.

Street signs are really only useful, though, if they're placed on the street. Many street signs are no longer needed, whether that's due to street redesign, age or damage. These street signs end up in metal surplus heaps and pawn shops, sometimes ending up in teenagers' bedrooms and school classrooms as decoration. Until you and your team of creatives came along, that is.

You will need a few things for this exercise: two other participants, some time, some motivation and access to available street signs (*not* stolen, of course!). The three of you are going to be creating a table using only street signs for materials. You will first need to collaborate to design what the table will look like and how it can be constructed. Consider the various shapes and sizes certain street signs offer, from the octagonal shape of a stop sign to the triangular shape of a yield sign, as well as the color of traditional signs. You can cut, bend, curve and rotate your signage metal to execute your design.

While many of you can and will stop here, we encourage you to find the street signs you would need to execute the design of your table, have the metal fabricated to the shape and size you need, go down to the hardware store and pick up the materials you would need and complete the table. It may take longer, but the collective result of building something together is worth the extra effort.

INTERVIEW: **ANN WILLOUGHBY**

Her mentor is Milton Glaser.
Her hero is Kevin Carroll.

Her agency just turned thirty years old, and her name is
Ann Willoughby. Ann is, most decidedly, a design icon by
all industry standards. She would passionately and humbly
deny as much, but in her denial even she must admit there
are few who have accomplished or experienced what she
has as a designer, as a teacher and as a person. She's both
engaging and curious, inspiring and humble. In short, she's
everything a young designer could aspire to be.

Even as we sort through all that Ann is, she's also a shop
owner. Willoughby Design Group recently celebrated its
30th anniversary; a mark any shop owner could attest is,
well, remarkable. What's the secret, Ann? How have you
managed to not only keep the doors open through thick
and thin, but do it with such creative power? How do you
keep it fresh and new and exciting year in and year out?
"The 'goosebump' moment," Ann would reply.

"We have a thing we call the 'goosebump'
moment. It's that moment when you and
your team are coming up with ideas, when
you're in the conceptual phase, and everyone gets goosebumps over a particular idea
or suggestion, when everyone knows that
the idea is perfect and right. We love the pursuit of that moment, and it drives us in every
project we work on."

Ann had been generating "goosebump" moments for three decades now, and while the makeup of her agency may have evolved over that time, the core values of her and her team have remained constant. "We've always felt that the real value in design for us is in the conceptual stage," Ann begins, "that's where you have the chance to do something special in terms of the implication of the solution, whether it's in the design or the message, or even in the materials that are used, and how those transcend the project and affect people. We like to stay involved in the materials we use in the design."

"For instance, we're helping a retail client of ours right now in continuing a relationship with a manufacturer of their bags to help them become a clean manufacturer. We don't want to order any more bags if they aren't eco-friendly. That has more to do with the relationship with the client more so than the process of the design, but we really feel that design is about improvement, and that improvement doesn't always stop at the door."

Much of the creative atmosphere at Willoughby can be attributed to the environment, but unlike most agencies, it's not just the studio. Those who are familiar with Willoughby know about the off-site environment that is as much a part of Willoughby's creative DNA as any other: the barn.

"I have a farm and I wanted a barn on our farm," Ann explains. "I've always loved the shape and space of barns. I rescued an old barn from Northern Missouri, wonderful 100-year-old timbers, just weathered and beautiful. We built it into our creative retreat. I love light, so we built the barn to have a lot of light, lots of windows and light-producing building materials. Even in the winter, the barn gets so much light, and it's such an inspiring place to be. It became a symbol for everything we stand for creatively. There's this real spiritual aspect to it, as you look out over the rolling hills, there's just something calming about it. We do everything out there, lots of entertaining and client meetings or sometimes just a place to get away and think. The barn is something that we built as a way of celebrating who we are as a company, really expressing it in a visual form. Our studio here is an extension of that same expression.

We really believe in the creative power of the environment, both outside and inside. **What you surround yourself with will affect both you and your team, positively or negatively."**

Along with the environment she's created, Ann has seen the positive effects of promoting creative thought through team-oriented outings and incentives. She admits "I like to bring in a masseuse about once a month and give everyone thirty minutes or so" to relax her team after or in preparation for a particularly stressful project, or provide time away to just be with her team. **"We have a fun day twice a year or so where we take off for the day, do anything from bowling to scavenger hunts.** People get all dressed up in costumes for them, too, it's so much fun. We have a committee that comes

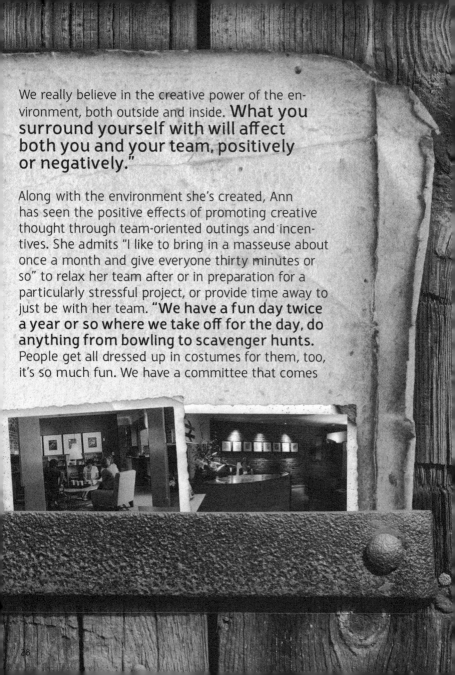

up with these things. I really think they get more enjoyment out of planning them than doing them!"

"Even changing up the usual hang-time, like the Christmas party last year was at a cooking school, where we watched them make the meals. When we were smaller and younger, we did a lot more active, spontaneous things. Now, we're sixteen people and folks have kids and are in the baby years so we have to plan a little more. People aren't as available as they used to be, but that doesn't change the need for some creative recharging. For instance, when people have to go out of town, whether it's for business or whatever, we'll often offer for them to stay an extra day and do some trend research and bring it back. It gives them an extra day to transition back into studio mode, take pictures of where they're at and be able to educate us on what they've learned."

Even while Ann is clearly the cornerstone of the studio, she still has an immense amount of respect and admiration for the team she's developed. "I think our greatest asset is the people here; they are an incredibly talented group of people; they work very hard at what they do. Without them, we wouldn't be where we are. The environment here is a great asset as well, we've tried to build a place that is inspiring and warm and comfortable, both in the people as well as the place."

Inspiring, warm and *comfortable*.

If there are three adjectives that better describe Ann Willoughby and her team, I don't know them.

Monsterblenderlicious

Halloween is the greatest holiday ever celebrated. (OK, that may be overstating things a bit, but go with me here.) It's the only holiday that not only excuses strange behavior and odd appearances, it encourages it. (My apologies to Thanksgiving at my brother's house and the unenviable encounters with Uncle Darren and his previously worn sock-puppet dramas.)

Today, to celebrate the spirit of Halloween, you and a partner are going to create a photo collage, digitally speaking. You need to combine three elements to make one crazy creature. You need to mix the celebrity of your choice, the monster or scary Halloween entity of your choice and the kitchen appliance of your choice to create the scariest celebsterpliance you can imagine. (Webster is turning in his grave, I know.) You and your partner each choose one of all three categories, then come together and share your three choices. Choose the "winner" of each of the three categories. Both of you then combine the three elements in your own ways to each make your monster.

Mold That Cricket

DreamWorks Animation SKG and Aardman Animations released one of my favorite animated films in 2006, *Flushed Away*. Claymation is a fantastic, if not time-consuming, technique for animation. The animators create characters that are so full of, well, character that they breathe life into a static object with both movement and design.

In the *Flushed Away* DVD bonus materials, an animator walks you through how to create one of the film's unsung heroes, the slug, out of ordinary modeling clay. Unless we are sculptors, animators, teachers or the like, we don't work much with modeling clay, but it's a fantastic medium to have some fun and create something unique.

You'll need to purchase some modeling clay for this project (or, in a pinch, run down to the local toy store and pick up some varying colors of Play-Doh). You and two partners will be creating a character out of clay, but with a twist. The three of you need to come to an agreement and choose one of the following themes to base your characters on:

Space
The wild, wild West
A safari
A pirate's life
Your studio/office
Halloween
The circus

Once you have chosen your group theme, each of you is to create a character or sculpture from that theme. It can be as large or small as you like or have time for. The only restriction is it must have something to do with the chosen theme.

My Bass Drum Is a Yawn

As creatives, we find our inspiration in a variety of places. Many creatives have credited their environments with being a huge influence in their work—everything from the intelligent design of manufactured goods to the artistic value found in the design of nature. If we'd be willing to open our eyes to what we see and hear every day and "re-see" our daily lives, we'd be amazed at what we've been missing all these years.

That's your task today. Choose to either "listen" or "see" and create.

Listen

This is a two-part exercise. Each of you is to use an audio recording device of some kind that can record and digitize ambient sound (like an analog or digital audio recorder, a digital handheld camcorder with a mic, or a tape recorder that can be digitized). Your task is to record sounds from everyday life. Record different types of sounds, manmade and natural, from city sounds to wind through trees. Try to isolate individual sounds. Once you've recorded and digitized the sounds, reconvene to start the second half of the exercise.

Choose one of you to start, and put the other participants in any order you'd like. Each participant will need to have access to sound-editing software when it is his or her turn. The first participant will use one of the recorded sounds to create a rhythm or repeating sound. After creating a few seconds of rhythm, give the file to the next participant. This participant will add a rhythm from his or her own recorded sounds "over the top" of the first beat to add to the rhythm, then pass it along to the next person, and so on. Each time, add one particular sound to add to the rhythm. You can agree to add one sound from each of your recordings or continue to pass it along and layer sounds as many times as you like.

See

This is a two-part exercise. Each of you will need a digital camera and access to photo-editing software for this exercise. Go out and take pictures of objects from everyday life in your office, in the park, on the street, in your living room, along the highway ... anywhere you find everyday life happening! You are going to be creating a "visual rhythm," so choose pictures of objects that can be isolated.

Choose one of you to start, and put the other participants in any order you'd like. The first participant is to create the "base" of the visual rhythm by taking one of the objects he or she photographed and duplicating it or laying it out in such a way as to create a basic linear repeating pattern, like the visualization of a bass line in a song. Once the first person is done, pass the file to the next person, who is to "layer" one of his or her elements over the previous pattern to add to the rhythm, and so on.

For instance, imagine the first participant took a picture of rolling hills. He might lay down the rolling hills as the bass line. The next person, in response to the rolling hills, might isolate an image she shot of a tree, and lay out four consecutive, evenly spaced images of that tree. The next participant might choose his image of a flock of birds and overlay them evenly across the "visual rhythm." You get the idea. You can add one image from each participant's shots, or continue to pass it along and layer images as many times as you'd like.

Ice Cream Hollandaise

As adults, we are accustomed to certain foods being categorized by mealtime. If we asked you to put a meal of scrambled eggs, bacon and toast under breakfast, lunch or dinner, we're sure you could manage to find the right place. Does that mean that we eat scrambled eggs, bacon and toast only during breakfast? Of course not, but that's the likely place for such a meal.

Give an eight-year-old that same power and you're likely to get back every manageable combination of candy and ice cream, regardless of time of day. Most older kids, however, generally know what food items should be listed under what mealtimes, but that wouldn't stop them, consequences aside, from adding a little extra choice to each category. That will be your task today.

In teams of three, create a menu based on items that kids would offer. In short, if kids created a menu for a restaurant, what would that menu be? Divide up the three mealtime categories (breakfast, lunch, dinner) among the three of you and create the menu that kids would create if they were running the show. (If ice cream doesn't show up in each category, you most likely don't understand kids!)

Happy Pantonium Day

If you're familiar with the hit TV sitcom *Seinfeld*, you're probably familiar with George Costanza's invented holiday, Festivus, and all the holiday rituals and traditions that came with it. (If you're unfamiliar with the episode or the concept, you can get the Wiki skinny at http://en.wikipedia.org/wiki/Festivus.)

Today, your goal is for you and a partner to create the "design" (or insert your chosen profession here) holiday, along with its traditions, rituals, celebration date, practices and details. The only restriction is that it should have something to do with design. Simply write it out in story or paragraph form.

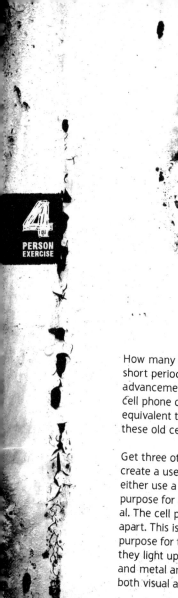

Cell Mates

How many cell phones have we had in our lifetime? In such a short period of time, financial independence or technological advancement has led us to purchase the latest and greatest cell phone or PDA. Recycling old cell phones has become the equivalent to recycling cans in the 1990s. What to do with all these old cell phones? Glad you asked.

Get three other partners for this exercise and collaborate to create a use for all of these abandoned cell phones. You can either use a set amount of cell phones or you can develop a purpose for all of them. Your solution can be artistic or industrial. The cell phones can be charged or dead, complete or taken apart. This isn't about recycling or removal, it's about finding a purpose for them. Consider their shape closed and open, that they light up and have screens, that they are made of plastic and metal and that they can receive and transmit. They are both visual and audible, and could be altered or disassembled.

We're Off to See the Wizard

You're not in Kansas anymore. The classic tale of Dorothy and Toto searching for a way home from the fantasy land of Oz presents four characters that we all can relate to, in one way or another.

Your task today is to do more than relate to those four characters, it's to become one. Grab a camera and three partners, and take a picture of your group. After taking the picture, print it out and one at a time, draw the cowardly lion, the tin man, the scarecrow or Dorothy over the top of a group member of your choice. When you have completed your sketch, pass the image to the next person, who will choose another character to draw over a blank group member. Continue until the entire group has been represented. Now, off to see the Wizard with you...

37

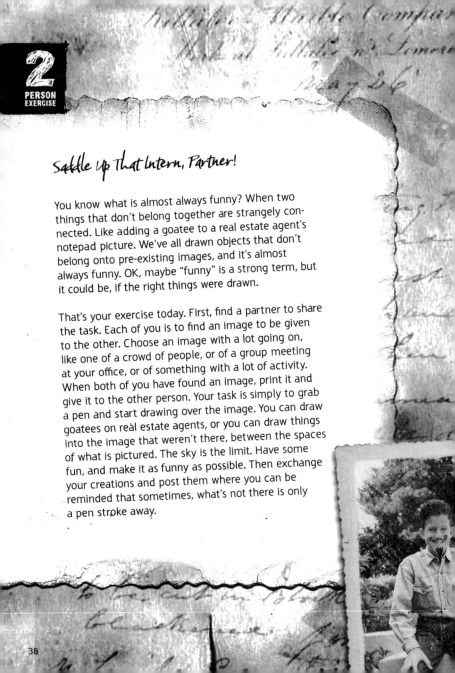

Saddle Up That Intern, Partner!

You know what is almost always funny? When two things that don't belong together are strangely connected. Like adding a goatee to a real estate agent's notepad picture. We've all drawn objects that don't belong onto pre-existing images, and it's almost always funny. OK, maybe "funny" is a strong term, but it could be, if the right things were drawn.

That's your exercise today. First, find a partner to share the task. Each of you is to find an image to be given to the other. Choose an image with a lot going on, like one of a crowd of people, or of a group meeting at your office, or of something with a lot of activity. When both of you have found an image, print it and give it to the other person. Your task is simply to grab a pen and start drawing over the image. You can draw goatees on real estate agents, or you can draw things into the image that weren't there, between the spaces of what is pictured. The sky is the limit. Have some fun, and make it as funny as possible. Then exchange your creations and post them where you can be reminded that sometimes, what's not there is only a pen stroke away.

It's a Pterodactyl! Awww! Awww!

Origami is the ancient Japanese art of paper folding. The idea is to create something recognizable by folding paper into geometric shapes and avoiding the use of glue or other adhesives. It takes a little patience to create something amazing, but what doesn't?

Today, you and three partners are going to engage in a little origami, just for the fun of it. First, choose a theme that the four of you will use as your base. It can be animals, space, under the sea, whatever. Next, go to www.origami.com and choose "diagrams," then "diagram list." From that list, each of you should choose a diagram to create that falls within the theme you picked. Follow the instructions on the diagram, and have fun!

39

INTERVIEW WITH

Chris Duh
KALEIDOSCOPE

Imagine a magical place where kids get the opportunity to freely and openly explore their creative selves and make things from paper and string, ribbon and tape, cardboard and markers. A place that invites children to make priceless works of art from melted crayons, design and create their own jigsaw puzzles, make paper hats and fold paper airplanes. Imagine a place where kids sit on giant caterpillars to create beautiful illustrations, enter an undersea world in the belly of a cat-adorned submarine and take flight in their very own fluorescent spaceship to create whatever they like. Now raise your hands if *you* want to go there and play. (You can all put your hands down.)

You don't have to imagine such a place. It exists. The next time you find yourself in Kansas City, Missouri, you'll want to set aside some time to experience it. This remarkable place is called Kaleidoscope, and it's a gift to the community from Kansas City's long-time resident corporate caretaker, Hallmark. The person in charge of Kaleidoscope's creativity-inducing design is artist and visionary Chris Duh. Chris has been an integral part of Kaleidoscope's design team for the last fifteen years, and he is dedicated to maintaining the creative vision passed down from the very top of the Hallmark food chain.

"Kaleidoscope started in 1969 by Don Hall, Sr., the son of J.C. Hall, who started Hallmark," Chris begins. "Don Hall, Sr., wanted to give something back to the community. He had extraordinary resources available to him in the form of scrap material left over from Hallmark's primary business. With a combination of smart business strategy and a heart for the Kansas City community, he began looking at what he could do to release some of these materials back into the community that would have a positive influence on the kids of Kansas City. He decided to build a test environment, keeping it on the Hallmark campus, a place where kids could come and create artwork for artwork's sake,

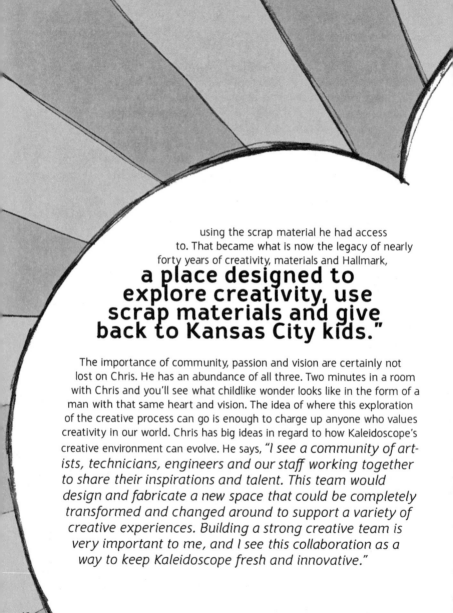

using the scrap material he had access to. That became what is now the legacy of nearly forty years of creativity, materials and Hallmark,

a place designed to explore creativity, use scrap materials and give back to Kansas City kids."

The importance of community, passion and vision are certainly not lost on Chris. He has an abundance of all three. Two minutes in a room with Chris and you'll see what childlike wonder looks like in the form of a man with that same heart and vision. The idea of where this exploration of the creative process can go is enough to charge up anyone who values creativity in our world. Chris has big ideas in regard to how Kaleidoscope's creative environment can evolve. He says, "*I see a community of artists, technicians, engineers and our staff working together to share their inspirations and talent. This team would design and fabricate a new space that could be completely transformed and changed around to support a variety of creative experiences. Building a strong creative team is very important to me, and I see this collaboration as a way to keep Kaleidoscope fresh and innovative.*"

You would think that this type of vision would be easily attainable, as any creative with even the remotest passion for the process would be able to get on board with the development of such a place. **What is so unique about Kaleidoscope and the team responsible for its ongoing operation is the absence of the primary purpose we, as professional creatives, usually work for: making money.** Kaleidoscope is offered to the community for free. They receive funding from the Hallmark Corporate Foundation to cover their yearly budget. *It's an interesting paradox when money is removed as a gauge of success,* and the vision of the growth of Kaleidoscope is left purposely open. What happens when client deadlines are replaced with open-ended vision?

What creative wouldn't jump at the chance to work in an environment that had virtually no hard deadlines? We all would say that would be creative nirvana, but hold on a sec. Chris has discovered there are unique challenges on that end of the spectrum. "The real quandary," Chris admits, "is how to evaluate what the success of a group is in terms of driving a business that is about creativity and not dollars. **Anyone, on any team, needs to know what their role is, what they're working toward and what constitutes success on a daily and visionary level.** Motivation becomes difficult when you can't look at a bottom line or when pressure doesn't exist to move things forward. We are not a financial group that is losing funds or is failing to meet a quota. Our basic quota is the amount of kids that we see, and that keeps increasing incrementally. So it's just a different rationale in the way we do business.

"Our small team is really good at performing the daily duties that keep Kaleidoscope running smoothly. The challenge lies in efficiently uniting our resources and making a commitment toward a shared creative mission. It is my passion to encourage others to take healthy risks, to explore their own creativity on a deeper level and to embrace experimentation and work through our failures. I believe it's invaluable that we all share the same vision and use the creative core within us to see it through, with the intent to make the ordinary extraordinary."

It's one thing to recognize the need to instill self-motivation; it's another to take the steps necessary to do just that. It requires a dedication to that process and a willingness to give up some of your own process to accomplish it. "Getting people to get past the natural human reaction of 'I can't paint like that, I can't design like that, I can't come up with ideas like that, I'm not going to talk anymore, I'm not going to engage anymore' is difficult," Chris says. *"But in order to reach any goal, the team has to feel not only included, but needed. It requires taking an inventory of what everyone's strengths are and how to use those to achieve the goal.* For instance, there have been two times that we've done these big projects: the full redesign of Kaleidoscope and the full redesign of the traveling exhibit. I tried to create projects that embraced our staff's individual strengths. Projects like papier-mâché, welding, painting. This allowed everyone to be involved and participate in the creative vision and execution.

Group ownership is key to group motivation.

That process of creating projects that involve and engage and communicate with one another openly about our own experiences is so important to reaching the goal. That's how I see Kaleidoscope: this incredible place where we have dialogue constantly about what we're building and work together, sharing and exploring our creative talents.

"For me personally, recognizing that finding a place for each person to have a creative voice, it's for me to say less and do less and letting the team participate more. Engaging in conversations about what our team would love for something to be like... to go through the uncertainties of feeling like they can't contribute to getting to a place where they can contribute, that has to be our measure of success," Chris adds.

We should all be so fortunate to gauge success by that standard. And it would serve us all well to find a Chris Duh to be around, even for a short time. **A reminder that to see the world through a child's eyes can have no ill effect on our creative soul, that's for sure.**

2
PERSON EXERCISE

Should the Racetrack be in the Front or Back?

You see it in the movies all the time, and we know there are incredibly wealthy jet-setters around the globe that have them, yet very few of us have ever seen the interior of them. From dignitaries to "international men of mystery" ("Smashing, baby!"), customized airplane interiors are the ultimate in luxury. How many times have you sat stuffed in coach, nestled between two "aromatic" travelers, and dreamed of having your own plane, complete with custom interior designed especially for you and by you? OK, maybe not that many times, but it sure is fun to dream! That dream becomes a visual reality today.

Get a partner for this exercise. Your task is to create the perfect airplane interior for the both of you. Discuss what should be in it, what would be useful for you both and how the plane would be designed inside. It can be a single level or double level, a 747 or a personal jet, it's completely up to you. Either draw the interior or list the details.

Staring at the Turkey in the Blender All Day

While there are many factors that play a part in our daily attitude or creative barometer, there is an underlooked avenue of creative expression that plays a role in how we feel about what we do every day, and simply altering that piece can make the immediate and near future a little creatively brighter: the desktop background on your computer.

Today, you and two of your desktop-wielding cohorts are going to create a new desktop background for each of you. But there's one small restriction. It has to include each of these elements:

A kitchen appliance
A Thanksgiving dinner dish or item
Something with fur
A strange fruit
A famous quote from a movie
An unfamiliar illustrated character

Each of you will start with a predefined desktop image size (like 1024 x 768, 1280 x 1024 or 1600 x 1024) and create the start of the desktop pattern using one of the categories above. When each person is complete, send the backgrounds to the next person, each sending and receiving a background from one another, and add another element from the list above. You can choose to stay in the same category or use an object from another category.

When you are complete, send it to the next person so all three people playing along will have an opportunity to add their own perspectives to the backgrounds. When complete, pass each back to the original background starter and apply them to your desktops. Prepare in advance the explanation to your boss. Feel free to blame the others—it's the corporate way!

Destroy This!

In every office, there's an "it." "It" is the one machine that is so loathed and despised for its noncompliance or complexity of use that we all want to go *Office Space* on it and annihilate it with a baseball bat in the middle of some field where no one can hear it scream. For some, it's a printer, for others, it's a copier or fax machine or computer. Regardless of your "it," there are times when you're caught daydreaming of how to best exorcise yourself of its evil. Now, you'll get your chance.

With four or more participants, you will be "chaining" a series of destruction scenarios for your "it." Start by creating a small book or notepad with as many pages as you are willing to offer destruction methods. Next, start by describing, on the first page, a possible destruction method for your "it." If you're searching for an appropriate starting point, throwing it off of the roof onto the street below is a fairly ubiquitous beginning.

Next, give the book to the next person in the chain, who is to add to the next page another possible destruction method, passing the book to the next person when the description is complete. You can either stop when all of you have had one chance to add your method, or you can continue to go around over and over if you're particularly demented today, or if your "it" simply deserves more.

4
PERSON
EXERCISE

It's Aliiiive!

Among the many things you can learn from Stefan Bucher's Daily Monster exercise (at www.dailymonster.com, if you're not familiar with the creative, cool experience) is that making monsters is fun! Today, you and two partners are going to make a monster, but you're going to do it one part at a time, and independent of one another.

Each of you should have a blank piece of paper. Assign who will be doing the head, the torso and the legs. Line the pages up vertically and put small tick marks at the areas that they cross to define where the neck will end and where the torso and legs will match up. From there, each of you will create your part of a monster. No rules—whatever kind of monster you want. When you all get done, line the pages back up and see what kind of twisted people you really are!

Your Table Fits My Earwax Collection Perfectly

A table's purpose isn't difficult to deduce. It's perfectly horizontal, it's flat and it's relatively sturdy. Therefore, it makes a great surface to put things on. Just imagine the types of things you could put on a table. You could put a glass, or a computer or paper. Wow, there's a virtual cornucopia of things you could put on a table!

The type of things you would put on a table largely depends on what type of table it is. A dining table is meant to have elements of dining on it, a poker table is meant to hold poker goods, a massage table is meant to...well, you get the picture. When the creators of these tables invented them, they started with a need, then created a table to satisfy the need (what a novel idea!). That's going to be your task today.

Today, you and a partner will be creating a table for a specific purpose. First, you need to define the purpose. Each of you will define the purpose of the other person's table. It can be a studio table that is meant to house every imaginable artistic tool, it can be a household table meant to provide liquid refreshment for the big game, who knows! Each of you develop a purpose for the other's table, then swap and sketch out the perfect table for the purpose you've been given.

Surprise Ending

We have all been privy to the "surprise ending," when a story we are engaged in takes an unexpected turn at the end. They incite conversation and recollection, as we struggle to remember key scenes and clues to this sudden turn of events. Twists and turns are engaging techniques used by storytellers to capture the imagination and attention of their audience.

Advertising uses this same technique, providing an image or story with no context, then "paying it off" with the headline and service or product being advertised. With such vague context, there are many "payoffs" that can be derived, if we take the specific product or service out of the equation. That is our task today.

This exercise is done as a chain, meaning you and three partners will be doing this exercise one at a time and in order. First, establish the chain order (who is first, who is second, etc.). The first person in the chain is to choose a vague image that is taken out of context. This image can be photographed, or it can be a found image. The image should be vague enough that many "payoffs" or headlines could be used to describe its meaning. Give this image to the next person in the chain. That person's task is to write the headline (payoff) and product or service that this new ad is for. That person then sends her solution and a new vague image to the next person in the chain, who is to do the same for this new image, and so on until the chain returns to the originator, who sends around or prints the solutions for all to see.

For instance, the first person might choose an image of someone sitting on the copier making copies. Sending the image to the next person, that person may write a witty headline for window cleaner, then send the new window cleaner ad along with another vague image (perhaps a new car on the side of the road with all four tires missing) to the next person in the chain, who might create a headline for public transportation.

Just like a great story, the more surprising the ending is, the more it's remembered!

4
PERSON
EXERCISE

Good Luck Starting With That

3
PERSON EXERCISE

Beginning, middle and end: the three basic parts to any story (actually, it's the three basic parts to anything). An ending does no good without knowing the beginning, does it? What good would it do to be given the page of a book that says, "...and after that odd event, the two parted. The end"? We are a society bent on answers, and to have answers, we have to know the questions. Today, you and two partners are going to create some of both.

Each person will need a digital camera. This will be a three-part exercise, with each person participating in each part, but for a different project. You will be creating a story that will consist of three pictures. Well, you'll be creating three stories, actually. The idea is that one person is responsible for taking a picture of something that will act as the beginning of the story. The next person, after seeing the beginning picture, goes out and takes a picture of his interpretation of what would come next in the story. After seeing both the beginning and the middle picture, the last person concludes the story by taking a picture of her interpretation of the end.

For example, let's say person one takes a picture of a full trash can. Person two, having seen the photo of the full trash can, might take a picture of a garbage truck. Person three sees both the first and second picture, and concludes the story by photographing an empty trash can. This is a bit expected, but you get the picture.

To add a level of complexity everyone pines for, you're going to be creating three stories at once. Each of you will be taking a different photo that is to act as the beginning photo. Then, switch photos and take the middle shots. Switch one last time and take the ending shots. Every person should have shot a beginning, a middle and an end.

My head hurts now. Think I'll go take a picture of an aspirin bottle. Then a couch. Then me smiling...

That's the Happiest Porcupine I've Ever Seen

My daughter was recently working on a school project, a poster with the subject "How I help my family be happy." She decided she wanted to take pictures of each family member (cats included) and write under the picture why that person is happy and what she does to help that. I told her under my picture, she should write "Daddy said he'd be happier if I were a boy." (I'm just kidding, people! Stop throwing things at me!)

We took pictures of all the family members, happy and smiling. The cats, however, wouldn't smile. She didn't like this. So I worked a little Photoshop magic and put a human smile, all toothy and grinny, onto each of the cats. She loved it, and I got a strange satisfaction and joy from the pictures as well. There's something about putting an unusual smile on something that shouldn't have one that's slightly creepy but funny, nonetheless. And it does represent everything that is good about doing what we do.

That's your exercise today. You and a partner will each choose a subject to make "happy." It can be an animal, an inanimate object, whatever you like. Find and send an image of your subject to your partner. Put a big, toothy grin on the image your partner sent you, and then send it back to your partner. This is guaranteed to make you smile, too!

Chicken to Stocking in Four Pics

4
PERSON
EXERCISE

We've all played "Word Association," the quick-hitting game where you blurt out the first word that comes to mind when someone offers a word as a guide. Played in a group, the results can be funny, especially if any beverages of a fermented nature are involved. One word after another, as quickly as possible, and you'll have no idea how one person can start with "sock" and five words later arrive at "rutabaga."

We're going to play a little association today, but not with words. We're going to play with pictures. This exercise works best with four to eight participants, enough to get the pictures back and be able to remember where you last offered your interpretation. It also works best when all participants know it's coming and have acknowledged they are participating. It stalls when one person isn't available to play and the rest don't know it, because this exercise is done through e-mail, which makes it great if your participants aren't in the same area.

Start by establishing your e-mail chain and letting everyone know the proper order (I e-mail Trevor, Trevor e-mails Corey, Corey e-mails Wendy, etc.). Next, choose an image and e-mail it to the first person in the chain; no explanation or guidance should accompany it. The person who receives the e-mail is to look at the image and attach the next picture in the chain. For instance, if the original picture was a chicken, a logical addition would be a picture of an egg, then maybe the Easter Bunny, then maybe Santa, then maybe a Christmas stocking. Each person attaches an image and e-mails it only to the person he or she is assigned, not to the whole group. This is important, as when it comes to each person, you are presented with the chain before you fresh and can enjoy the perspective!

You can decide ahead of time how many times it goes around. But be wary of the power of the Internet and the twisted minds of creatives!

55

2
PERSON
EXERCISE

Creative Director to William Four. Check

The game we know as chess originated in India in the sixth century with ties to military divisions and formations. Today, millions of people play the game wrought with strategy and cool-looking pieces. While traditional chess pieces carry visual associations to their rightful names (pawn, rook, knight, bishop, queen and king), more festive variations can be created to replace them, if the mood should strike. Ouch! Hey, the mood just struck!

You and a partner will be creating chess pieces based on people you know. They can be people at your agency or place of business, famous people or simply friends and family. You must collaborate to define what group of people will be used, and then the fun begins. One person takes white, one person takes black. Each of you will create your own chess pieces based on the chosen group, whether it's written, sketched on paper, rendered digitally, molded from clay or built from other materials. It's your choice who you target is and how you build it. When complete, reconvene with your pieces and, if they are physical pieces, play a game. Just be careful if you check your mom. She gets grumpy when she's backed into a corner.

Wise Is the New Young

They say the older you are, the wiser you've become. I think my Grandpa Donald is the glaring exception to that, but don't tell him that. (Or go ahead and tell him. I'm sure he'd hear the word "wise" and gum through a New York mob story about a wiseguy he beat up in "the good ol' days" anyway.) It's clear that wise isn't solely owned by the age-impaired, as we have all learned something in our years of creative service. Everyone has learned little nuggets of wisdom to pass down to the creative toddlers biting your ankles.

Today, you and a partner will be creating a list of the top ten things you've learned so far in your profession of choice. Each of you should develop your own list of ten, then combine your lists and edit to make the comprehensive official ten things. By being authentic and humorous, and keeping the list real and lighthearted, you'll be sure to pass on memorable advice to the ankle-biters.

I Grew a Whole Crop of Interns

Wouldn't it be great if we could grow designers, photographers, illustrators, writers and the like? We could go down to the nursery, pick up a couple of skill sets that we don't personally have, spend a Saturday in the backyard and presto! We'd have our own creative team that could round out the areas we struggle in. Well, now you can! Sort of.

Your task today is to invent "creative seeds." Just the packets, but it's a step! Take the names of each person in your group and randomly draw them so each person gets a different name. Your task is to draw, sketch, digitally create or illustrate the packet of seeds used to make the person whose name you drew. If the person is a designer, you're making "designer seeds." If the person is a photographer, you're making "photographer seeds." Be sure to include what "extras" will bloom when the seedlings have grown to the size they are now.

You Are Now Free to Move Around the Gymnasium

While there have been significant trides made in the design of commercial bus interiors, the fact is that most are built to accommodate dozens of passengers, their luggage and the necessities, like a driver. Only über-successful rock bands and well-known football commentators can afford their own private buses to hit the open road in style...until now. Have you ever dreamed what it would be like to have your own tour bus? If you had an unlimited amount of money, and you were required to spend it on building the perfect luxury tour bus for you, what would it be like? That's the task today, but it's not just for you, it's for you and two partners.

Brainstorm, on your own, design features and creature comforts you would have on your own bus. After you've jotted down a few ideas, come back together, share your ideas and design the bus interior on paper. When you're done, start saving and you should be able to build it around 2187.

Watch the Road!

If you travel along any paved roadway in just about any urban area on the planet, you will be confronted with one of the most basic forms of commercial communication: the billboard. These outdoor staples of advertising peddle everything from fast-food delights to mortuary services. Anyone who wishes to advertise anything to a group of people in transit is welcome in this space, and what a large space it is!

Your task today is to create a billboard. Not the visual representation of the billboard, but the actual billboard, too. You and a partner will be creating a miniature billboard, designed to advertise to a group of people who perhaps were spared of these urban monstrosities. First, choose a theme for your billboard from the list below:

Medieval knights academy

Sporting goods for the first Olympics

Egyptian mummification tools and accessories **Prehistoric camping grounds**

Gladiator battles at the Colosseum

Mozart's concert tour

Each team of two is to develop their "subject" or creative direction from the theme, then work to create a miniature version of the billboard from whatever materials you'd like. Use paper, cardboard, Popsicle sticks, barbecue skewers, presentation board, foamcore, whatever you'd like to build a replica of your billboard. Have some fun by setting a time limit. (If access to building materials is present, an hour to ninety minutes is a great time frame to push creative execution.)

I Have a Guitar Pick High Flush

Since the twelfth century, folks have been playing games with cards. From solitaire to Texas Hold'em, we love card games. One of the reasons, of course, are the cool suits! What's not to love about hearts, diamonds, clubs and spades? The shapes are so engrained in our collective playful psyche that just the mention of the words incites shouts of "I'm all-in!" (Oh, is that just us?) Regardless of what game you play, the cards are the same. It's time for that to change.

4 PERSON EXERCISE

You and three partners will be redesigning the four common suits of playing cards. Choose a theme below as your design guide:

Rock 'n' roll
Childhood toys
Junk food
House party
Ugly
Tacky
Baseball
Ancient Egypt
Cartoons
Video games

Each person gets a suit based on the overall theme you've chosen. Your suit can be full color, or you can stick to the traditional red and black. Design your suit marker and what the ace and five card of your suit would look like. If you're feeling snappy, design a whole deck based on your four new suits.

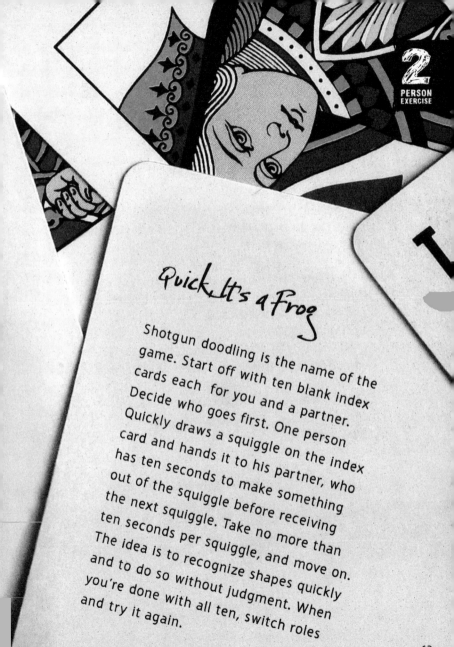

Quick, It's a Frog

Shotgun doodling is the name of the game. Start off with ten blank index cards each for you and a partner. Decide who goes first. One person quickly draws a squiggle on the index card and hands it to his partner, who has ten seconds to make something out of the squiggle before receiving the next squiggle. Take no more than ten seconds per squiggle, and move on. The idea is to recognize shapes quickly and to do so without judgment. When you're done with all ten, switch roles and try it again.

The Remote's in the Crisper

A thousand full-size refrigerators. That's what you have. Don't ask us where you got them, but there they are in your backyard. A thousand of them. Some still work (you think). What are you going to do with all of them? That's for you and a partner to decide. **Collaborate to come up with twenty ways to use a thousand refrigerators.** But there's one catch: You can't use them as refrigerators. They can all be used together as part of something bigger, or they can be used separately, but you'll have to come up with how you're going to use all one thousand of them. Write your solutions out on a piece of paper, or if you're feeling especially spicy, get artistic and draw it out.

My Cell Phone Charger Fits Nicely Next to Your Ketchup Stain

Everything is a pat-
tern. Even random can
be a pattern if the random is
repeated (boy, that's deep). Our world
is full of pattern; it just takes a keen eye to
recognize it. Have you checked your eye lately?
Is it keen? Sweet! You're ready to find some pattern. Or,
better yet, make some pattern.

You and two partners will each take a picture of something
in your own personal space. The more random the image is,
the better. After snapping the pictures, print them out and
lay them on the table. The task is to collaborate to create
a pattern out of the parts or the whole of all three pictures.
You can either use the pictures in their entireties to make the
pattern, or you could take elements of the pictures and combine them together to make the pattern. Print up multiple
copies of the images, and either arrange or cut up the images
to make your repeating pattern.

3

PERSON EXERCISE

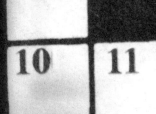

"I Wonder if I Can Dig a Tunnel to the Copier From Here," Tom Thought

Ever wonder what your coworkers were thinking? Of course not. Most of the time, you know anyway, don't you? It's time to prove it with a little playful imagination. Grab two fellow mind readers and let's show everyone what they're thinking.

You'll each need a small piece of thin plexiglass, at least the size of a piece of paper. You can get this at any hardware store. Find a place in your environment that you can see a few of your coworkers' work areas. Each participant in the exercise should choose a different place within your environment. Hold the plexiglass up in a spot that encompasses the coworkers' areas. With a dry-erase marker, draw talk or thought bubbles coming from your coworkers. (Talk or thought bubbles are commonly used in comics to indicate someone talking or thinking. Talking usually has a pointer or arrow pointing to the person speaking, while thinking usually is indicated with small circles leading from the person to the thought.)

Once you have your talk or thought bubbles drawn, turn the plexiglass over and use a permanent marker to trace the bubbles more accurately. When you have completed the trace, erase the dry-erase bubbles away from the other side. Fill in the words or thoughts from your coworkers with a dry-erase pen and let everyone know what they are thinking.

If you want to take it a step further, build a stand for the plexiglass so that anyone walking by can participate in the conversation by writing in his or her own idea of what's going on. One more step and you might make the plexiglass larger to encompass the whole area, allowing people to draw who-knows-what over people's work spaces...

25

3 Down: The Sound Trevor Makes When E-Mail Is Down

In 1913, a Liverpool journalist named Arthur Wynne published what is accepted as the first crossword puzzle. Since then, *The New York Times*, Simon & Schuster and a host of other publishing companies have been challenging the world's wordsmiths with the black-and-white grids.

Players are generally attracted to puzzle subjects that they have some experience in, which is precisely what you will be engaging in today. You and three crossword compatriots will be creating crossword puzzles based on your work environment. Each of you is to create a puzzle that has at least six horizontal and six vertical intersecting words. Each of you will create your own, then return to the group to exchange puzzles and solve them. Start by writing down a list of words you could use, like people's names, terms that are familiar in the environment, recognizable places, common objects or client relations. Then assemble your puzzle structure. Lastly, create the clues that your team will need to figure out your puzzle.

Turn That Frown Upside Down!
Now Add Projectile Vomit...

Have you ever had one of those moments when you saw someone who was incredibly attractive, then he did or said one thing, and all that beauty went out the window and he was instantly unattractive? OK, maybe it's just me. But if you can at least imagine it, it will help to visualize this exercise.

Grab one other willing participant, a few sheets of blank paper and some pencils (use pencils, as you may want to erase something along the way). Choose one person to start as the initiator (don't worry, you'll be taking turns). The initiator is to draw an object that is happy, attractive, cute, joyful or generally positive. When complete, the other participant is to change one thing about that drawing to make it the opposite.

For instance, imagine one of you drew a cute, happy squirrel. The other participant could choose to add devil's horns and turn it to the squirrel from Hell. You get the idea. Take turns drawing something happy and the other changing one thing to make it the opposite, then flip it and start with something unhappy and change one thing to make it good again.

Yeah, Baby, Yeah, Yeah, Baby, Yeah

4 PERSON EXERCISE

Ever wonder how people write songs? Some of the lyrics are either so absurd that there's no way they were conjured by a human brain, or they're so brilliant that it's impossible to imagine someone could write that powerfully. We're going for the absurd part today, but we also understand there's **a fine line between absurd and brilliant.**

Grab three other budding lyricists. You and your partners are going to write a song today, one line/verse/chorus at a time. First, decide whether you want to write it verse by verse or line by line, and whether you want to write the whole song or just the chorus. Next, designate the order in which you'll write. The first person writes either one line of a verse, one line of the chorus or the entire chorus. The next person writes the next line or verse and so on until you've reached musical nirvana and are submitting unsolicited songs to LeAnn Rimes. Continue the cycle until the entire song is complete. And at least try to rhyme!

Cockroaches Can't Run From the Pencil-Flinger!

It's widely known and scientifically proven that cockroaches have been in existence before Earth was invented (scientific research not included). But regardless of their history, the fact remains that very few people like cock-roaches, and even fewer people want them in their houses. The myriad of cockroach repellants on the market are evidence that people will do just about anything to get rid of the suckers. You and a partner are going to grab a piece of the repellant pie today.

Your task is to create a cockroach repel-lant (or "remover," if you catch our drift). You must create this repellant from the items you can see right now, and the items can't be chemically based. The goal is for you and your partner to cre-ate a cockroach solution from everyday objects, then market your repellant in the form of packaging and a print ad. You both should collaborate to decide what the solution is and what it should be called. One of you takes the packag-ing design and the other takes the print ad. You can create the items digitally, you could draw the items in as crude a way as you like, or you simply could write the solutions on paper and explain them verbally when you return to your group. Happy hunting!

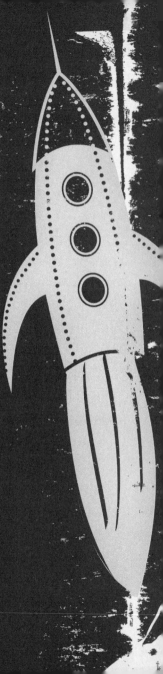

Don't Ask Aliens If They Know Will Smith

**It happens all the time. Aliens land and abduct
a few hapless humans for experiments.** That old
chestnut. The question isn't whether it will happen to you,
it's what will you do when it happens. Someone needs
to create the Official Alien Abduction Dos and Don'ts list.
You have some time right now, so why don't you and that
person over there put that together. Collaborate to develop the things you should and shouldn't do when you're
abducted by aliens. Just make sure the aliens don't see it.
Hey! That's number one!

Interview With
JUSTIN AHRENS

RULE 29

Design is communal. The very purpose of design is a conversation and, as such, involves more than just ourselves. *While the artist within us wants to make the idea and the execution of that idea solely ours, the act of bringing other people into the process multiplies that idea's chances of growing larger than ourselves, and big ideas are what we're supposed to be about.* Learning to work together to accomplish a shared vision is a tougher task than it should be, but a few enlightened souls have discovered that coming together produces ideas that are far greater than anything they could do alone.

Justin Ahrens is one of them.

Justin is the head honcho at Rule29, a Chicago-area design firm bent on "making creative matter." He has successfully taken this collaborative philosophy and formed his agency with an eye on getting together to solve problems. "When I first started," Justin begins, *"I was doing your average production stuff, and the way I progressed from that was attempting to collaborate to do anything I could with the art directors there, just because I was so hungry to learn.* That sort of became a style of mine as I grew. I would find artists and photographers whom I admired and had work they needed done, and I would help them out, but it was really for my own benefit. *I was learning about the stuff they looked for and how they liked to be talked to from an art director standpoint.*

"Fast forward several years later when I was looking to start Rule29. I did it not only to get to work on the type of things I liked, but also to have the ability to work with anyone who would want to work with me. Starting in 2000, I called a bunch of photographers I had worked with in the past, along with a paper company and a printer I had a great relationship with, and I asked everyone, 'What can we do together to help each other equally, but also create an amazing piece?' So the photographers donated images in return for product samples that they could send out, the same with the paper company and the printer, and that's been the formula we've been developing over the last eight years. Every year now, we do several projects like that instead of just one. It's really exciting.

"When we retooled in 2003, we decided we'd go after the types of clients we'd want to work with, but we also decided we were going to do two or three collaborative projects a year. The second I made that decision, I was simultaneously working on two amazing projects with people around the country. I started to think that maybe I could tool the agency's workflow in the same collaborative way. I've dealt with the situations that arise within an agency team and the political positioning that occurs, and **I thought that if I could set it up as an open environment where everyone felt they had a voice but everyone was drinking the same Kool-Aid, we could do work that was very collaborative and very rewarding.** If you got stuck, you could pass work around and not only would it not lose strength, it would gain strength because you saw all the different perspectives play a role in the outcome."

The "collaborative team of individuals" model, like any model, has its strengths and its weaknesses. The concept of group ownership of ideas is a difficult pill for many designers to swallow, as we're so protective over our ideas and our solutions. Justin's ability to trust the team he has assembled is what has turned out to be the key to its success. "Culture is so important in this model," Justin reveals. *"One thing I learned starting out doing things this way was if the project was well defined in the beginning and we were able to trust each other to do our parts, that's when it worked the best. The projects that I micro-managed or were loosely defined, those projects didn't turn out as well. You have to trust the process and the team within it.*

This process shouldn't be foreign to designers. We work with copywriters and photographers and printers and illustrators on almost every project we do, so the concept of collaboration isn't new to us. It should be innate to us, but for some reason, when it comes to working with another design firm, or working with your internal team, it often isn't as smooth as you would think it should be. That's the role the leader plays, bringing together the right people and establishing the right culture."

Rule29 has been evolving this model and working in their own unique creative process. Their process isn't unlike many agency processes; they have just defined a few areas within it that highlight the collaborative nature of their philosophy and empower the people within it to develop the most effective, creative ideas they can. Justin explains, **"When we start a project, we'll start with a creative brief meeting that the whole team attends. Everyone at Rule29 has different abilities, and sometimes I might put people with skill levels that are outside on the core of the project in leadership positions just to give it a fresh perspective, and they end up designing some of our most innovative stuff.** At the meeting, I'll give some direction or some sketches, and the designers will go off and start absorbing the research and initial ideas.

"Depending on the size of the project, we often create an image board of found imagery that represents the character of the project, everything from who will be viewing it, to typography styles, to illustration styles if it's an illustration project, photography or video styles, and we present the board to the team. That usually starts the ideation process and people start kicking out ideas. Then we start to get into idea development. As the designers begin developing ideas, they'll bring me in on it, show me the concepts, I might have a thought or two of feedback as they complete their idea development. Then we'll have a critique that everyone is involved in.

"We always have a devil's advocate in our critiques who is in charge of hammering on the project. He asks the tough questions, like 'How does this fit with our strategy? How will it communicate to the end user?' As the ideators, we have to support or defend the idea against this scrutiny. **The critique allows everyone to see what everyone else is doing and be able to learn from one another.** Sometimes, designers get stuck. Because of the collaborative environment we've built, we have the ability to switch projects and get a new perspective into the work.

We can have someone else take that project to the next stage and have another critique. The environment allows us to be agile and exploratory, knowing we can get multiple inputs on the strength of the idea and the execution. The studio manager here keeps us all on schedule, because we know that everyone works differently, and we want to allow that freedom without sacrificing anything on the project."

Within this process, Rule29 provides three distinct collaborative moments where group ideation is featured, none of which is more unique than the "Mojo Meeting."

"We have three 'idea-generating' times throughout our process," Justin imparts, "and each serve a unique purpose. First, we have that initial creative brief meeting, where ideas get thrown around, and usually, that meeting serves to throw out the off-the-cuff, expected ideas, the stuff that represents the low-hanging fruit. After the first critique, we'll have another brainstorm after we've had the opportunity to see the ideas. We'll talk about what we can push or what we can do more.

"Either before or after that initial critique, we have what we call the 'Mojo Meeting.' Our goal with this is to say, 'What can we do for this specific client?' It really has little to do with the project we're working on; it's entirely big ideas about the client's business. There are no rules; it's not an assigned project. It's simply ways we can help our client in their business. As a side benefit, we often find great extensions for the projects we're currently working on. *Other times, it's just an exercise for us to use to get out all the fantastic ideas that aren't necessarily on strategy for the project we're working on.* Our clients see that we spend time thinking about them, not just their project, and occasionally, budgets mysteriously appear and we actually get to produce some of the fantastic ideas we come up with."

It's clear that Justin's approach to the creative process and a passionate belief in the power of the collaborative idea has led to great corporate success. But it's in this passionate belief that he has developed something that, like his work, is greater than himself. **He's developed unity, and in this business, bringing together a group of people that can truly say they are completely engaged in the vision is more valuable than anything that can be achieved without them.**

Mine Is of an Empty Coffee Cup

3
PERSON EXERCISE

They say a picture is worth a thousand words, but could it be worth twenty-four hours? While one picture can do a lot, could it describe your entire day? How about part of your day? We're about to find out.

You and two partners are each going to take one picture that encapsulates part of your morning, afternoon and evening. Take one picture for each part that will completely sum up that part of your day. When you reconvene, put all the pictures on the table in a big pile and invite someone not in the group to come in and try to put the three pictures in order for each person.

Watch My Biker Jump Chapter Three

The most basic form of animation is stop-motion. This is a technique that calls for taking a still photo of a three-dimensional scene, moving the subjects in the smallest measure, then taking another photo and so on. When the photos are shown in rapid succession, the illusion of fluid movement is perceived.

Another term for this technique is flipbook animation. We've all probably experimented with flipbook-style animation, even if it was on the corners of the notebooks we were supposed to be keeping notes in during biology class. It involves drawing a simple subject, then on the next page, drawing that same subject one small measure of movement forward, and so on, until we have multiple pages of our subject engaged in the illusion of movement.

Today, you and a partner are going to create a flipbook in two chapters, the "before" and the "after." First, the two of you need to choose a theme for your animation from the list below:

**An office disaster
A bad meal idea
Hanging Christmas lights
Home improvement
An impromptu race
Computer trouble
The carnival**

After choosing your theme, choose one of you to be the "before" and the other to be the "after." You'll now need the paper for your flipbook.

You can choose to purchase a blank notepad for the exercise, staple sheets of printer paper together, or use the corner of an existing notepad as your medium. The person selected to be the "before" will be setting up the scene. Use as many sheets as you need to communicate the scene. Set up the scene by creating the scenario that your partner will complete. Stop just short of determining what will happen with the scenario you've created.

For instance, if your theme was "bowling mishaps," the "before" animator might create a stick figure that steps up to the ball return to pick up his ball to bowl his first frame. As the stick figure holds the ball up in preparation, you stop and turn the flipbook over to your partner, who will complete the animation by determining what occurs from this point on. If it doesn't end in some atrocity, you're not thinking big enough!

You Hate It When I Do That

We all have pet peeves,
those little things that others do that seem
to set us on edge. They're usually small and
insignificant to others, but it just presses our hot
buttons when we experience them. To some, it might
be when people mispronounce their name. To others, it may
be when people talk on their cell phones in movies or on elevators.
To some, it's just an annoyance, but to others, it's a full-fledged pet peeve.

Of course, we know our own pet peeves, and we may know most or all of
someone else's pet peeves. (In some instances, we may even *be* someone else's
pet peeve!) Today, you're going to explore just that—someone else's pet peeves.
Get a partner and list ten pet peeves...of your partner. Some might be real based
on what you know of the person, but some are going to be fictional, also based on
what you know of your partner. Take what you know of your partner and create ten
pet peeves you may know or think he or she possesses. They don't have to be the
big, obvious ones (*No one* likes people talking on their cell phones in movies).
You can invent strange, peculiar pet peeves based on what you know
of your partner's personality.

Rock Band, Volume Three

If you haven't played the video game Rock Band from MTV Games yet, put this book down right now, grab those leather pants we know you still have from college, go down to your local game store and rock! In the game, players play three "instruments" in a fake rock band. There's something intoxicating about the rock band fantasy. The urge to rock is in all of us. Even that guy in accounting. And it's certainly in you.

In honor of those about to rock, **your task today is to create makeshift instruments and flat-out rock.** Each member of the group is to create a different instrument out of materials you have at your disposal right now. You'll at least need a front man with a microphone, a lead guitar shredder, the soulful bass player (or tinny sax player, if Michael Bolton is more your style) and a drummer. Each member of the band is to create his or her own instrument. When you're done, **START ROCKIN'!**

Where Did You Find That Trash Can?

4
PERSON EXERCISE

Scavenger hunts rock. Admit it, you love them. You are trying to be cool right now, aren't you? Don't worry, we know you love them because everyone loves them. You are going to engage in a little scavenger hunt for today's task.

Everyone will need a digital camera. Each of you will have a list of terms that you must go out into your assigned area and shoot your idea of those terms. Each person is shooting or providing one image per term below:

Passion Gross
Overused **Brave**
Pressure Smelly
This isn't going to end well
No one will know Scary
Victory

When you return, print up each of the photos and group them on the wall to create your very own term collages.

... And Then, William the Intern Exploded. The End.

Have you ever seen a strange photo that made little sense until either the caption was revealed or an explanation was given? Advertising makes a living out of strange images that make little sense without the caption explaining the product or service. Imagine a children's book written in a language you don't understand. Think you could decipher what was being said based on the images? You're about to find out just how difficult, and funny, that process can be.

Download and print this PDF:

www.wakeupmybrain.com/CftCT/storypaper.pdf

Assemble, fold and staple the sheets along the dotted lines to create a small booklet that has blank pages on the left and lined pages on the right. Between you and a partner, elect one person to be the illustrator and one person to be the writer. (Don't be intimidated by the term "illustrator." It's just the person elected to draw the pictures; they can be amazing colored drawings or as simple as stick figures if you want!) The illustrator is up first. On the left side of the booklet, draw six pictures of a story. You may have a story in mind, or they may be random. Use no words or captions, and explain nothing to the writer in your team. When you have completed drawing on each of the six blank left-side pages, give the booklet to the writer. The writer is to look at the drawings and form a story based on what he sees. Either try to figure out what the illustrator was saying in the drawings, or make up a story completely from your perspective of what's going on. Who knows, there may be a children's book or airplane crash survival manual in your future!

Crappy Idea Ornaments

If you're like us, you have a whole trash can full of bad ideas. The idea goes down on paper, is rightfully and globally mocked for its terribility and horrendousness, and is then wadded up and tossed in the can. With so many wadded-up balls of crappy concepts, and an ecologically minded disposition, there has to be a way to recycle all those bad ideas, right? Right! You and a partner are going to come up with a really good idea for all those really bad ideas.

This is a "shotgun" exercise, in that you are going to come up with many ideas very quickly, without valuing them or judging their validity, one right after another. Designate one person as the writer. Both of you begin generating ideas—just start spilling them out, without consequence and without judgment. The writer is to write one idea down on each sheet of paper, move it aside, then write the next one. Do this until you have twenty or thirty ideas written down.

Go back through each of the ideas, talking about whether they are viable, could be done, would be fun to do, etc. Come up with what you both deem the best idea. The others are to be wadded up and thrown in an empty wastebasket. (You better be shooting these from a distance and keeping score!)

Now's the hard part. Take the one idea that is left...and do it. You have a wastepaper basket full of bad ideas just waiting for your great idea to save them!

I'm Sorry, Sir.
Your Ear Looks Like
a "G," and I Need
a Picture of It.

Ever see a cloud that looks like the letter "C"? Or a shadow cast from a group of trees that looked like the letter "M"? Sure you have. Who hasn't? If you haven't, maybe you haven't been looking hard enough. Letterforms are everywhere, if we're willing to find them (and occasionally modify something here or there).

You and two partners are to split up the letters in the alphabet equally (with one person getting the dreaded question mark to make it even). Your task is to take your digital cameras and find your letters made out of anything but actual letters. Look at shadows, look at buildings and shapes and patterns to find your letters. Just stay away from real printed letters. If you need to move something from time to time to help with the letters, go ahead, but try to find them naturally occurring. And which one of you has the letter "G"? Good luck!

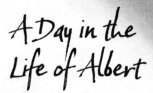

A Day in the Life of Albert

4 PERSON EXERCISE

Your day is filled with routine, sprinkled with unexpected surprises (are there any other kind?) and spontaneous twists. We know this because everyone's day can pretty much be described the same way. If they were going to make a documentary called "A Day in the Life of [insert your name here]," it would most likely prove our point. We're going to explore a little of this concept of "A Day in the Life," but not of you (that would be too easy). You're going to photograph a day in the life of someone else...without following the person.

Everyone on the team is to randomly draw the name of someone else on the team. Your task is to take a digital camera and photograph your interpretation of a day in the life of that person, based on what you know of him or her. Don't worry if you don't know that much about the person—you know *something* (physical features, at least) so you can improvise and photograph what you *think* a day in the life of him or her would be like. Take at least five pictures (ten would tell a better story, though). Return to the group with your "Day in the Life of" feature, and explain the glamour of the day!

You're So Twisted

We're all twisted, aren't we? Go ahead, you can admit it, we already know. You do what we do, which is silently twist any tale we are told when we are engaged in a story. When your bud at the desk next to you is telling you about the time he was riding his bike to work, you instantly think"...and your front wheel came off, throwing you into a face-plant on the sidewalk...uh, huh..." Yeah, we do it, too. It's usually more fun than the actual story anyway.

Today, you and a partner are going to have a little twisted fun by writing your own twisted story. First, decide who the "core storyteller" is; the other person will be the "twister." (You'll each get a chance to do both, so don't worry.) The "core storyteller" is to take a lined sheet of paper and start writing a story, but only on the first line. After the first line, give the paper to the "twister." That person's job is to write the next line of the story, but twist it to take an unexpected turn. Return the paper to the "core storyteller," who will write the next line in the story, but in a traditional way (no twists—just write what would logically come next in your mind). Return the paper to the "twister" to take the next line in the story and twist that, too. Continue for as long as you want, or until the story abruptly ends (which often happens when "twisters" are involved). Then switch roles and write another story. But, please, don't share these with anyone. You're liable to frighten those you love!

Office Graffiti Is No Longer Frowned Upon

There is a wall somewhere in your environment that needs some lovin'. (No, not that type of lovin'.) Like a blank canvas, it begs to be transformed into something beautiful or useful (or both). Often, whoever is nearest to the wall will benefit the most from it.

Grab two other participants for this exercise. The three of you are going to redesign one wall each. Grab a digital camera and take a picture of three separate walls in your environment that need some attention. The best-case scenario is that the walls are near the three people involved in the exercise. Exchange walls so that each person is working on someone else's wall. The task is to redesign the wall by adding to it, subtracting from it or using a hybrid of both. You can apply color, you can build something out from it, whatever you think would best utilize that particular space best. For some, that may mean a cool mural, for others, a full-fledged installation. You decide how to best tag that wall with what it needs.

The Perfect Whatever-You-Are

We all have people in our line of work that have certain talents we wish we had. Some people are naturally gifted at illustration or animation. Other people can somehow find the perfect angle and perfect lighting to photograph something you never saw to begin with. Regardless of our seemingly endless list of shortcomings, there is someone somewhere that looks at us in that same light. If there was just some way to take the best of a group of people and collect it all into one person, you'd have the perfect whatever-you-are. No time like the present to do just that!

Your task today is to create the ideal whatever-you-are out of the best traits of the group.

We say "whatever-you-are" because we know you're not all designers or illustrators or photographers. Tailor this exercise to create the best whatever-you-are. If you're doing this exercise as a group of funeral home attendants, then you're about to create the best funeral home attendant imaginable from the best traits of each person in the group.

4
PERSON
EXERCISE

One person needs to act as moderator and start the exercise by downloading and printing this starter image as large as possible:

www.wakeupmybrain.com/CftCT/perfectwhatever.pdf

Next, the moderator should take the names of everyone in the roup and disperse them randomly, so everyone has the name of someone else in the group. Write the one greatest talent or characteristic you feel the person whose name you have drawn possesses in relationship to your industry. It could be anything from "She can make a dead rat look beautiful in a photograph" to "I wish I had his energy"—whatever physical talent or personal character trait you feel is that person's strongest in the field you are in.

If your group has fewer than six people, write two talents or characteristics for each person to better complete the final image.

After everyone has completed a character analysis, each person is to add a visual representation to the downloaded starter image by drawing or noting in some way the talent or character trait. For instance, if one of the talents is "incredible ability to sketch," then perhaps drawing a pencil or pad on the starter image would be appropriate. If the character trait is "calm in the face of adversity," perhaps a can of antiperspirant or a book on Zen client dealings in the jacket pocket would do the trick. As you add your talent or trait, explain your reasoning to the group. When you're done, you'll have a great example of what your team looks like (or could look like) to the outside world.

Where'd That Flying Blender Come From?

Have you ever noticed that when Fred Flintstone is running inside his house, the same window goes by twelve times? How is that possible? How long is that man's house, anyway? Can you imagine sitting outside his house, watching him go by in each of those windows? His house must be a hundred yards long!

While Fred is basically in the same pose each time he passes, the idea of seeing something through consecutive windows makes an interesting look into visual storytelling. That will be your task today.

You and two partners will be telling a story out of, or into, three consecutive windows. First, decide what three consecutive windows you want to use, and take a picture of the three windows on one shot. You can choose to shoot from either the inside out or the outside in.

When you have taken the shot, print it out on a sheet of paper. Designate one person to start. That person's task is to draw something happening outside (or inside) the first window. It doesn't have to make a lot of sense; it can be quite random and still work well. After completing the drawing, pass the paper to the next person, who either tells the next chapter in the story in the second window or continues the image as if it's made its way to the second window. On completion, pass the picture to the last person, who completes the story in the third window. Just don't accuse the person of being a creative Peeping Tom!

You Made This Into That?

Ever been at a restaurant that lines the table with white butcher paper and provides a box of crayons? Is there anything better than dinner and a show, creative style? If you're anything like me, that table is completely filled with doodles and sketches and every creature imaginable. Embarrassingly enough, some of my best illustration work has been on a butcher paper tablecloth.

This exercise was born out of those creativity-inducing dining experiences. You and a partner are going to engage in a doodle-build. One person starts by doodling a random shape or mark on a piece paper. Then, the other person adds to the doodle by starting the process of turning it into something. Don't finish the work, just add the next step based on what you see. The first person then gets to add to it based on what he sees. Go back and forth until you're satisfied you've created the oddest drawing possible, then switch roles and let the other person start the doodle. **Stains count!**

... And Dave Finally Gives in and Agrees to Do It. Fade to Black.

Have you ever looked around your agency or business and thought, "This is like a movie"? OK, maybe not that often, but it could happen, especially if you're looking for it. Like investigating the world around you for visual detail and inspiration, searching your environment for the plot of a movie is just as unique. Watching how people interact, noting the power struggles within team members, amplifying character traits in people...all of these could lead to the next Hollywood blockbuster, if you're willing to look and listen.

Get a partner for your screenwriting debut. The two of you are going to chain write a movie script using your environment as the foundation. Start by writing the opening scene, a simple paragraph that starts the story off. Send this scene to your partner so he or she can add the next scene. Don't get too detailed, and limit dialogue to only what would be necessary to convey the story. Go back and forth adding scenes until you've reached a natural conclusion to the story, or until Martin Scorsese calls, whichever comes first.

Interview
with
Clint! Runge
from ARCHRIVAL

Creative challenges are one thing, as we all yearn for the opportunity to solve a problem, but some problems cross the line from "challenge" to "suicide." Imagine you've been given the task to capture the attention of a group of people with your ideas. You say, "No problem, I do it all the time." Add to that the need to not only capture their attention, but incite them to act. Again, your confidence does not waver. How about getting them to become brand evangelists for your client's product, sing its praises on the streets, knock down the door of the local retail establishment to make a purchase. That's getting a little tougher, huh? You say, "It depends on the audience. If they are willing participants, easily led, aren't very good at sniffing out corporate influence, then maybe. If they have the disposable income to make such purchases easily and if they listen and are obedient to the voice of authority telling them what to buy and when, then there's a chance."

Now imagine the target audience is eighteen-year-olds.

"I quit."

Normal reactions aside, there are those that specialize in communicating to that very audience and with those very intentions. While the age range may be a bit broader in actuality, the task is still monumental. Enter Archrival, a youth branding agency located in a place few would expect: Lincoln, Nebraska. But don't let the location fool you. *Archrival is proof that the coasts no longer hold the patent on perception-altering work.*

So geeked about the work they do is Creative Director Clint! Runge that the exclamation point found within his name is still not enough to accurately describe both the work and the shop he started with college pal Charlie Hull.

Their unique approach to reaching this elusive audience starts with the team they've assembled, and, like the audience to which they speak, they've valued diversity and authenticity above all.

"Our staff," Clint! begins, "is eighteen different types of creatives from all kinds of backgrounds: graphic design, advertising, marketing, architecture, animation, fine arts, interactive—a wide range of disciplines. This was a purposeful decision on our part; it speaks to the philosophy we have about approaching the work we do.

"Our studio takes a 'problem-solving' approach to our work, which may sound like a cliché, but we mean it slightly differently. For example, let's say there's a retail store that wants to sell more product. Based on what type of agency they hire, they'll get different type of solutions. If they hire an ad agency, that agency will say, 'We can improve your business; we're going to advertise for you— we can build you billboards, newspaper ads, magazine spreads,' which may or may not work. If that same retail store hired, say, an architecture firm instead, they might say, 'Let's redesign your store. We'll give you a whole new look.' The client could hire a graphic design firm, and they might say, 'We'll give you a whole new brand so you'll appeal to more customers.' Depending on which agency the client hires, the solution is going to be fairly one-dimensional. I guess that having a background in architecture, we always had a more philosophical approach. **The solution to a problem has to be all-encompassing.** When we hire creatives, we look for those people who specialize in an area, but have interests and skills in others. They may be coming from an advertising program, but they are really into design. Or they have an architecture background, but they love music. You put those kinds of people together in a room, I think it becomes really exciting. You might get a graphic designer working on a poster, but someone with an animation background will look at that poster and say, 'How does that poster move? How does it change over time?' Someone with an interactive degree may look at it and say, 'Do people interact with it? How do people touch posters? Do they get to do anything?' Then someone with an architecture background might say, 'What is the material of the poster? Where will it go? Does it have any dimension?' That's the heart of Archrival—the idea of always questioning."

With diversity comes a natural curiosity of other mediums certainly, but managing such a diverse staff has its challenges. Like all creative teams, there are times when creatives are just burnt out and need a different perspective. Managing a team of creatives often means seeing the rut coming and being proactive in heading it off. "We take a couple different approaches," Clint! explains. "One direction we'll take is redefining the problem. For example, we are doing some packaging for a beer client, and the first round of work we did was good, but it wasn't great. For round two, we decided to step back and learn more about beer and the brewing process. So we went back to where they brew, we took tours and drank their range of beers. It was fun, of course, but it was a learning experience as well. **By doing so, getting out of our normal environment and mixing research with fun, we found a new perspective and were able to redefine the problem.** It wasn't about what people would buy, but rather what people would enjoy. By doing just that, enjoying the product, we redefined the problem and were able to look at it from a different angle.

"Another approach we'll take is to give the team a break of responsible freedom. We let them take a three-day trip once a year where we pay for their basics—hotel, airfare, etc. We let them do whatever they want with the caveat that their purpose is to learn or grow creatively. They might be going to New York to study advertising in the subways, or to Vegas to study the design of the casino chips. We let them go do something they really want to do, and let them creatively splurge and have fun. When they come back, they are energized and recharged, and they tend to put that into the project.

"For example, on the beer packaging project, a couple of our guys wanted to go to Colorado, where this beer festival was being held. They had a great time, but they also saw a lot of beer and a lot of beer drinkers. They got to see how people

enjoy beer and when they came back, they were really inspired. We had to almost limit the number of ideas that they could work on simply because there was a time factor. But they were fired up, and to us, that's a win."

The combination of Archrival's client niche and the leadership's architectural background certainly has played a role in the physical development of the work environment. With environment playing such a huge role in creative energy, the space couldn't disappoint. "I love our space," Clint admits. **"Our goal was to have something that our team felt proud of, we wanted them to say, 'Hell yeah, I work here. I work at Archrival!' We believe that sense of pride translates into their work. We really feel that the space helps people to be more creative. Our team might spend fifty to sixty hours a week here—it has to help them.**

"The space itself is pretty wide open. When you are walking by somebody's computer screen, you can see what they are working on. It's a bit intimidating sometimes because you might be working on something that isn't fully fleshed out yet, there's a little adjustment, but afterwards people tend to really love it. Like I said earlier, when someone with an animation background walks by and asks a question, it might be just enough to push it to a new direction. From each desk, you can see and talk and ask questions. It's very communal.

"The materials in the space itself, we did a lot of fun Midwest-type stuff. We took an old truck out of a scrap heap and made it into our reception desk. Everyone's desk has a 'fence' between them. You can add slots to the fence to make it taller if you want to be a little more private to focus a little more on your project, or you can take slots off and you can be more public. We let everyone customize everything. They can put whatever they want. Whatever makes them inspired, go for it. Everyone is going to have their own flavor, and that's great."

It's no wonder Archrival is pumping out great piece after great piece. They remain authentic to their audience, they have developed a philosophy that works for their team and they have a bucketload of passion for what they do.

The exclamation point says so!

I Just Flipped Jeff's Tongue. Gross.

3
PERSON
EXERCISE

Light switches have a pretty simple purpose: to turn the lights **on** and **off**. For many of us, what we have to offer is often overlooked when people fail to see past our purposes.

In a creative meeting, we were throwing around ideas for a music-related client. We had to develop a new ad campaign for them, and we only had three days left before the presentation. Ideas were flying, but none of them had any tooth to them. We were circling the wagons, but we could never find the idea that would ring the bell. After an hour of hurling idea bombs at the wall, the office manager walked in to alert one of the designers of a phone call. After the designer left, the office manager slipped in to grab a stack of files left on the table. In a flippant tone, I asked her what kind of idea could we wrap this campaign around, and on her way out, she confidently spoke one line of an idea that squashed everything we were coming up with. She nailed it. From that day on, she was invited to every idea session we had. If we'll take the time to look past the purpose, we often see the blank canvas behind.

The purpose of a light switch is simple, but we fail to notice the canvas behind it: the plate. There's so much that can be done with the metaphor of a light switch, and there's even space to do it. That's your task today.

Get two other participants for the exercise. Collaborate to develop a theme for the light switches in your environment. Come up with something that has some meaning to your environment, then collaborate to develop ways you can execute (not electrocute!) those ideas and create masks for the light-switch plates. Swap them out when everyone is gone and see how many people notice the light-switch campaign you've just launched. If you need help, ask the office manager.

I Hurt Your Squiggle Bad

In *Caffeine for the Creative Mind*, we offered an exercise that asked you to take a series of lines and a circle and arrange them to visually represent words like pain, love and pressure. Today, we're going to take a similar approach, but with a twist.

Get one other participant for this exercise. Designate who is the artist and who is the interpreter (don't worry, you'll switch it up after the first time through). The artist is to draw a simple squiggle or a simple object. After drawing the squiggle or object, give the paper to the interpreter, who must change or modify that squiggle or object to visually represent one of the following words:

Painful
Dizzy
Angry
Stressed
Cold

The artist should draw a different squiggle or object for each interpretation, so at the end, the interpreter has used a different squiggle or object for each of the five words. When completed, switch roles and do it again.

We Made Chalk Welcome Mats in Front of Every Door

Orange County, California, is home to an amazing art festival, the Fun With Chalk Street Painting Festival. Sidewalk chalk artists from all over come to create amazing chalk art on the streets of Mission Viejo. The medium is difficult but rewarding, and walking along these masterpieces is breathtaking. There's something authentic about making a canvas from a surface we generally overlook every day. But not today.

This task, for you and a partner, is to buy a bucket of sidewalk chalk (you can pick one up at any toy store or art supply store) and create something on the streets of your environment. We know what you're saying: "We're not artists!" Yes, you are. You just haven't used your talent lately. Now's your chance. Collaborate to come up with a simple image or message that you can create on a street, and then spend a few hours and do it. Sometimes, the best creative igniter is to jump in with both feet.

I Got Smell!

Storytelling is at the heart of all communication. From brands
to music, the ability to tell a well-crafted story is one of the
purest art forms in history. Traditionally, though, we rarely use
more than two or three of our senses to tell a story. Imagine
if we could tell a story using all five senses. That would be a
powerful story! It's time to give it a shot.

You are going to tell a five-part story, using a different sense for
each part. The perfect number of participants for this exercise
naturally is five, but you can divide up the five senses any way
you need, with some taking on two or three parts to the story
as needed.

4
PERSON
EXERCISE

The first step is to develop a story that takes advantage of all
five senses. Collaborate as a group to develop your story along
one of these story lines:

The Agency Murder Mystery
Love Between Chefs
My Summer as a Rock 'n' Roll Roadie
Tailgating at the Super Bowl
The Florist and the Fly
Halloween Night
The Short Life of a Bee

Once the group has chosen a story line, start developing a story
that can be told in five parts, using the senses for each. For
instance, for the sense of sight, a photo or video could be used
for that part of the story. For the sense of smell, something
brought in that emits an odor could be used for that part. For
the sense of touch, something tactile would be used for that
part of the story, and so on.

Once you have developed your story and how each sense plays
a role in that part of the story, divide up and acquire each of
the things you need to tell the story. Reassemble with the
items and lay them out in some way to "tell" the story. Bring
in people not involved with the group and take them down the
line, letting them experience each part of the story using a different sense. Don't tell them what the story is; ask them to tell
you what the story is as they experience it. You can give them
the title of the story as a guide to the type of tale it is, but then
let them tell you what they are thinking as they go. If your story
uses chocolate chip cookies for one of the senses, be sure to
have plenty on hand!

Ha Ha, Dave's a Vegas Showgirl Dancer!

Many of us wear many hats at work. Not actually—that would be difficult—but figuratively, as there are many duties we need to perform. Sometimes, it's difficult to distinguish which hat we're wearing, so it's time to practice.

4
PERSON
EXERCISE

Break off into teams of four. Each team will need to take headshots and arrange them on a single sheet of paper. The idea is to cut off the tops of everyone's heads (again, not actually!) so that hats can be drawn on top. You can either do this digitally or by printing out the headshots, placing a piece of paper over the tops of the heads and photocopying the result. Make sure to leave enough room above everyone's heads to draw on the hats.

Pass a sheet of headshots around to each person in the group. Each person is to draw hats on all four head-shots based on one of the following themes:

Jobs needing to be done in the office
Fantasy occupations each person wishes he or she had
What each person wishes he or she were doing right now
Each person's historical equal

You can find hat images and digitally add them, cut from printed pictures and paste them to each person, or draw them on each headshot. And what you're planning to do to that guy over there is messed up, man!

Your Capital "L"
Overlapped My Thought Bubble

Letterpress is an incredible layering printing technique where impressions are created, inked and applied to receptive surfaces. The technique is beautiful and easily reproducible, as the raised surface can be inked multiple times. When overlaid, the result is artistic and fun. You and two partners will be creating a letterpress collaborating image right now.

3
PERSON EXERCISE

First, choose a theme for the group:

A designer's life for me
What I want to be when I grow up
Unbalanced nature
Monday morning   This is how it really is

Next, the three of you need to collaborate to come up with a three-part image—background, middle and foreground—that works for the theme you've chosen. The image should be simple, and you should be able to draw it in the three parts.

You'll need some art supplies to create the impressions. Pick up a few sheets of rubber, an ink roller and three stamp pads of different colors. You'll also need three wood blocks to which you will attach the rubber sheets.

Divide up the foreground, middle and background images to each of the participants. Draw the individual image, starting with the background, on a single sheet of rubber, remembering to draw it as its mirror opposite, as applying the image to paper will produce the right-reading positive. After completing the image, use an X-Acto knife or scissors to cut away the unused portion of the image, leaving only the image. Attach the image to the wood block, and roll the rubber stencil with one of the ink colors. Press the stencil to the paper to reveal the image.

When the ink has dried, the next person applies the "middle" image over the background image using the same process. Finish the piece by applying the foreground image. Stand back and marvel atcho bad selves!

My Camera Froze While Shooting the "Ice Ice Baby" Part

4
PERSON EXERCISE

In 1981, MTV brought music videos to the masses by starting the first twenty-four-hour music video TV channel. Since then, music videos have become a normal part of the commercial music landscape. Hordes of directors, producers and writers have cut their teeth on music videos.

You could write a music video, couldn't you? Aw, c'mon, you know you could. We know you could. As a matter of fact, you're going to prove it right now.

Grab at least three partners and between the four (or more) of you, choose a song for the group to use for the music video. Once you've decided on a song, divide up the chorus and the verses, each person getting one verse (or the chorus). When everyone has been given his or her respective lyrics, grab a digital camera (the picture kind, not the video kind) and head out into the music-video lovin' world to shoot an image (or series of images) to accompany each line of your verse or chorus. Print the images full page and reassemble for the screening of your new music video.

Hang all the photos on a wall or series of walls large enough to be able to put each verse or chorus in one horizontal line. When each person has put their images in the right order, play the song with each person pointing to the appropriate photo at the appropriate time in the song. When the song is complete, call MTV and let them know your agent is waiting.

My Body Is Definitely a Six-Eye Body

We're infatuated with monsters. We know it. What makes monsters so fun is that there isn't a right and wrong way to draw them. There isn't a monster model somewhere who defines what monsters are supposed to look like; they can look like anything we want. That's why they're monsters! You and a partner are going to draw some monsters right now.

One person will draw just the eyes for the monster. They can look like whatever you want, and they can be however big or small, few or many. After drawing the eyes, hand the paper to the other person, who is to take her cue from the eyes and draw the rest of the monster. Switch roles and do the exercise again.

PERSON EXERCISE

I Spelled "Make the Logo Bigger"

In June 2006, twelve creatives from Wieden+Kennedy in Portland, Oregon, purchased 150,000 boxes of clear pushpins. Using the pushpins, they built a fourteen-foot mural that simply said "Fail Harder," a tribute to the philosophy of the creative director of the twelve. As remarkable as the feat was, it would have been lost if the words said "Make More Money" or "Design Rocks!" It was the simple but jarring message along with the execution that made it such a memorable piece.

Today, you and three partners will be doing something similar (although you'll need no pushpins, so the local office supply store need not be alerted). Each of you will need a camera for this exercise. But first, come together and decide on

a theme. Make the theme have meaning to your group, the way the "Fail Harder" message had meaning to the twelve Portland creatives. It can be in relation to your place of business, to a principle or theory we creatives value—anything vague enough to have personal perspective for each of you, yet have community meaning for the group.

When that theme has been established, each of you is to come up with your own word or term that describes or points to that theme. When you've decided on your word or term, grab your camera, go out into the community and shoot found typography for each letter of your word or term. When you've shot each letter separately, use your computer to assemble the pictures together to spell out the word or term. You'll have to crop the images to put the letters close enough together to be read. Reassemble and share your creations.

3

PERSON
EXERCISE

That Tape Roll Makes Great Horns

Hollywood does it all the time. They use shadow to imply an ominous creature is just around the corner, only to find two trees came together to cast a shadow in the exact shape of the serial murderer **THAT'S RIGHT BEHIND YOU!!** Whew, that was close. Shadows are a great way to communicate that things aren't always what they appear. We're going to play a little with shadows today.

Get two other willing participants for this exercise. The three of you are going to be casting a shadow of a scary monster on the wall or floor, but you're going to be creating that monster from found objects in the room. First, you'll need a light source, such as a desk lamp or a floor lamp that can be directed. Next, use only objects in your immediate space to create a sculpture that, when light is cast from behind it, shines your monster's shadow on the floor. Now, set it up around a corner and wait for an unsuspecting victim to pass by!

Wanna Go Play on the Cosmigraphotron?

When's the last time you went to a playground? Seriously? The playground equipment is virtually the same as when I was a kid (I know, I know..."but horses and buggies are expensive, son..."). Today, kids play virtual reality video games; they have handheld devices that play movies, games and music, wash the dog and clean their rooms for them. Technology is more a part of a kid's life than ours, as they haven't experienced anything different...except for their playgrounds. How can exercise and fitness and social interaction compete with entertainment centers that fit in their pockets? That's for you to decide today!

Get at least three partners. Together, you will be creating a playground built for today's kids. You have everything and anything at your disposal. Each of you will create your own apparatus, and you will put them all together to make the playground. Keep in mind the various climates and ages the playground needs to endure. Either describe with words or draw with pictures your part of the perfect playground for today's kids.

3

PERSON
EXERCISE

This Month Is "Punch a Vendor" Month

Calendars are a big December business. Everyone and their mother wants the new year's calendar. (OK, maybe more their mother than them, but you get the point.) The choices are endless, from wrinkly puppies to wrinkly people. The core of the calendar is the same—it's the joy of turning the month over on the first to see the surprise of another wrinkly puppy that everyone likes. But maybe you don't like wrinkly puppies, and neither does your team. You like other stuff. You want to hang a calendar that says something about you, the pride you have in your environment or industry, and the unadulterated joy you have in creating a calendar. We know, we feel you, dog!

That's your task today. Get two other participants for this exercise. The three of you will be creating a calendar for your environment or industry. First, decide what the subject of the calendar will be. It can be your agency or firm, it can be your industry, it can be wrinkly puppies (but that's been covered already). Next, split up the months so each of you gets four months.

Each month needs different artwork and a different type of calendar setup. You can find a gazillion types online, or you can make your own. You can create the artwork in any fashion you like—photography, illustration, stick figures, hieroglyphics…whatever works for you. Work in the official holidays to the calendar, and add a few unofficial holidays. There's always a reason to celebrate something!

The Message in the Bottle Said, "Leave a New Message for Someone Else"

Guerilla art, as Keri Smith describes it in her book *The Guerilla Art Kit*, is "leaving art and ideas in public places where you can affect someone's day, change their mood or their mind, and maybe even change the world in the process." Advertising agencies have been using guerilla marketing techniques to peddle their clients' wares for decades now, but the idea of creating guerilla art simply for the betterment of humankind is an admirable endeavor, and one you and three compatriots are going to engage in today.

The four of you are to collaborate on a guerilla art project that you will execute on a street level. It can be anything from chalk quotes on sidewalks, to impromptu scavenger hunts leading to encouraging messages, to creating a message in the loops of a chain-link fence. Take a look at your environment, develop a message you want to convey and head out to execute it. One piece of advice: the more surprising the message is, the more powerful it will be, so executing it in the stealth of night or when people aren't around will have a greater effect than executing it when they are around.

4

PERSON EXERCISE

X Marks the Spot, But So Does That Repeating Crisscross Pattern

Following a map to buried treasure is an adventure we'd all love to embark on. Following clues, dodging dangers, opening the chest...it's all good! But to creatives, treasure doesn't have to be gold doubloons or emerald-encrusted dishware; it could be a really good photograph, a distressed font on a wall or inspiration you hadn't experienced before. Emerald-encrusted dishware is nice, too, but for the sake of our exercise, let's go with the unexpected inspiration.

You will need at least two teams of two people for this exercise. **The task is to create a treasure map of photographs to be taken along the way.** It would be best to do it outside in your community, but if need be, it can be done inside your environment. Each team should go out into the community and map out certain things to be photographed, keeping track of ways to move the other team into position to see these photographic subjects. It can be done with steps and turns, such as "Take sixteen steps, turn left, take a picture of a pattern you see," or it can be done in other ways. The idea is to present the other team with six to eight photographic challenges or subjects that perhaps get overlooked in your community. At the end of the map, have some definitive message or shot that they can use to know they have reached the end.

Each team is to prepare a map, then exchange the maps and go out and execute the photographs. Return to show what you have found. **Arrrr...**

My Dog Ate the Logo

The dog ate your homework. You were abducted by aliens. Homework is against your religion. Homework is institutionalizing America's youth, and you won't stand for it. We had all kinds of excuses for not doing our homework when we were young, didn't we? Where did all that lying, cheating, mischievous creativity go? We got responsible, that's what happened. I say, let it out again! In my design class, I tell my students that if they are late with an assignment, the only thing that gets them grace is if they come to me with the most creative excuse they can. A lame excuse (or worse, the *truth*) can only serve to lower their grade. I have yet to be disappointed.

It's too bad our workplace can't be as forgiving. Maybe the problem has been we simply haven't developed creative-enough excuses. Time to remedy that. Grab a partner who is familiar with your daily work environment to help with the exercise. Your goal is to develop creative excuses for five common deadline-driven scenarios in your work environment. First, you'll need to decide which five scenarios need excuses. It may be why you're late to a meeting, or why you missed a deadline to show comps to your CD, or even why the comps you are showing to the client are missing the logo. Come up with the scenarios you are most likely to experience, then develop the most creative excuses that explain the result. If your dog ate the logo, you get a "D."

Name:
Dave Gouveia
AND
Chris Elkerton
If lost, please return to:
3DogZ
CREATIVE INC

On any given Tuesday morning, you're likely to find every single member of a particular Toronto-based design shop huddled around the creative director's monitor. From the client's side of the desk, you might think they are engaged in design theory over a specific creative challenge found within a recent project, or maybe offering their own unique brand of perspective toward a colleague's work. However, a trip to the business side of the table would find the banter of design critique giving way to the laughter of movie critique as they spend the morning filtering through the newest batch of online cinematic releases.

Welcome to 3 Dogz Creative.

Proof that you don't need a huge agency to develop huge ideas, Creative Directors Dave Gouveia and Chris Elkerton, along with Account Manager Roberta Judge, started 3 Dogz Creative after commiserating together at a larger shop. "We started this," Dave begins, "because we were all working at this larger agency that was, how shall I say it, 'unsupportive' of our work. **We wanted to do it our way.**" And so they did, producing award-winning work from the time the doors opened.

Along with the "3 Dogz," they have one full-time staffer and a revolving door of juniors, freelancers and interns to round out the team. With a group so eclectic and small, how do they maintain such a high level of creative firepower? **"We don't have big heads,"** Chris offers. "Any one of us, from juniors and interns all the way up our long and prestigious corporate ladder to me and Dave, can critique each other's work. There's not this air of superiority where we are the CDs and they are the employees or the politics of some stupid design pissing contest. We can learn just as much from our employees as they can from us. The environment here is very open. We just want to do really good work; we don't care who creates it."

Dave adds, "I am constantly asking for advice from our employees. They have a perspective that I don't have, so if they see something or have something to add, I want them to. Now, I don't have to listen to them, but I want them to say something if they have something."

"A collaborative setup is so much better than a competitive setup," Chris finishes. "We just get so much more from each other when we're working together versus if we were trying to beat each other."

So what is it about this collaborative, small-headed environment that seemingly pumps out great idea after great idea? **"Attitude,"** Dave surmises. "We know that every one of us works differently, our process is different, how we go about generating and executing ideas is unique. We don't try to force anyone to work a particular way. We want our employees—and ourselves, for that matter—to be able to work the way we work best. Then it's Chris' and my job to take all these different ways of working and bring it all together to produce the best work we can."

Chris jumps in, "We have a pretty loose shop, we take summer hours ("because summer's only twelve weeks long here, we gotta do something!" Dave interjects) we go out and have a beer after work, we like hanging out with everyone. It's so much easier when everyone has the same sense of humor. When the same things are funny, it's easy to laugh."

Dave adds, "Not that we don't have any discipline whatsoever. Let's be honest, in the end, we're a business and we have to be able to get the work done. One of the best things we ever did was begin setting and hitting internal deadlines. **As long as we create and strive to make our own internal deadlines throughout a project, it frees everyone up to work however they like.** I have a tendency to wait until the last minute to do something, whereas others here are rifling through forty thumbnail comps a week ahead of time. By setting the internal deadlines, we can all work how we work best, and the projects never suffer."

While the project timelines may be disciplined, it's clear the creative energy at 3 Dogz is completely untamed. A portfolio full of incredibly good work and a shelf full of industry awards is the calling card of a group of people who are not only good at what they do, but love it just as much. Dave summarizes it perfectly: "We actually like what we do and who we do it with, and that attitude allows us to let everyone here work how they work best."

Finding clients who recognize and appreciate that attitude hasn't been too terribly difficult. Their approach is infectious. But while not all clients are perfect fits for their style, they have their fair share who are completely on board with the vibe. "We know which clients we can say 'Hey, motherf'er!' to and which ones we can't," Chris says.

I'm sure we all have a few we'd like to say that to, Chris.

DAVE

Roberta

CHRIS

Look! Jill Is Headfirst in John's Pocket!

We often take photos that use perspective as a prop. For instance, if you have visited the Italian town of Pisa, who hasn't stood across the grass and taken a picture that looks like you're holding up the Leaning Tower? Or at the Statue of Liberty, standing on the opposite shore, it's common to take a picture as if you're tickling Lady Liberty under her arm. Perspective can be fun to play with, especially in two-dimensional mediums. Like what you're going to do today.

Grab two other partners for this exercise. You will be snapping three scenes, one where each of you plays the central role. One of you will be taking the picture, one will be the subject and the third will be the perspective object. Find a place or setting where you can use perspective to have the subject and the object interact in an unusual way. For example, it may be set up so it looks like the object is small and standing in the palm of the subject's hand. Come up with a unique situation for each shot.

That's Not a Drawing, That's Just a Sausage Stain

Most California Pizza Kitchens, the casual dining restaurant chain started in 1985 in Beverly Hills, California, have walls decorated by artwork created by painting on pizza boxes. Sometimes these pizza boxes are stand-alone paintings, and sometimes they are grouped together to form larger canvases. As beautiful as they are, they make a wonderful analogy for individual life.

Each of those boxes is closed, and the outside of the box is painted beautifully. The inside of the box, however, holds a secret. We can only see the beauty on the outside; we have no idea what the inside holds.

4
PERSON
EXERCISE

Each of us is like those pizza-box paintings. We have an outside mask that we wear, what the world sees of us, but few people have ever seen the inside of our pizza box, the place where we keep what we really want to be. The greatness within us lies confined by the mask we wear. It's time people found out who we really want to be.

Each of you will need to procure a blank pizza box (unused, hope-fully). The small size will most likely work best, and the sturdier the better. Most pizza boxes have pizza slogans on the outside, so if you can't find blanks at your local pizza store, a coat or two of gesso from your local art supply store would work to provide that outside canvas.

On the outside of your box, draw, paint, write, collage or illustrate what your mask is, what the world sees of you. It can be one char-acter trait, many traits, your physical being or a more meaningful representation. On the inside of the pizza box, draw, paint, write, collage or illustrate who it is you want to be. It's not a representa-tion of who you really are, it's who you really want to be. It will have more meaning if it's tied either in style or substance to what's on the outside of your pizza box.

Reconvene when you are complete to share your pizza boxes, perhaps over pizza!

Luke, I Am Your Milk-Carton-Faced Father

TO OPEN

Remember when you were in grade school, and arts-and-crafts time usually meant taking some form of everyday object and making a Mother's Day present out of it? Mom still has the paper plate sunflower, doesn't she? Good times.

There's something to that "everyday object" stuff. Finding different things to make out of everyday objects presents an interesting creative challenge. Take, for instance, the typical half-gallon milk carton. It's rectangular, modifiable and light, and it has two distinctly shaped ends. It's just begging to made into something. But what? The choices are endless. So pick one!

Grab another willing participant for this exercise. First, each of you is to write down your own list of ten things you could make out of your standard cardboard half-gallon milk carton. They can be anything from children's toys to practical uses. Then, when both lists have been completed, exchange lists and choose one of the items from the list to execute and make. It will require you to acquire the milk cartons, but after doing so, go to town on the item you've chosen. You might want to rinse them out first: no use crying over spoiled milk!

I Can't Find a Word For "Still Lives At Home"

In 2007, three students in a senior-level visual arts class at BYU created the opening credits to the Typophile Film Fest 4. They created a three-minute story of a person's life by using typography as the vehicle, starting with little Ys trying to swim into the center of an O, and ending with the typography of a death certificate, with amazing typographic artistry in between. (You can view the film here: http://typophile.com/node/45002.)

4
PERSON EXERCISE

The concept is incredible and literally brings to life the power of typography in our day and age. Today, you're going to use typography to tell a story.

This exercise is done chain-style, where one person starts the chain with an image and passes it to the next person, who adds to the chain and passes it on. The goal is to build a story of single words, one right after another. To do this, you will be taking pictures of found typography, words you have found out in the world. A rudimentary example might be a picture of the word "birth" written on a birth certificate, then a picture of the word "life" written on the box of a board game, then a picture of the word "death" graffitied across a brick wall.

The story will build over time, with no defined direction. Start by taking a picture of a found word. Give the picture to the next person in the chain. She is to find a word that she feels would go next in the story and photograph it. Either staple the new photo to the first photo, or e-mail the photos to the next person in the chain. You can do this over the course of a predefined period of time, or a certain number of rotations through the group.

The Conference Table Is Made of Highlighters

There's one room in your environment that needs some help. We know it, we've seen it. No one uses that room as much as they would if it were designed a little better. Maybe it needs some furniture, maybe the usage of the room doesn't fit its size. Whatever the challenge, you and your creative caffeine partners know how to make the room perfect. You're not interior designers (or maybe you are!) but you know what would work, what the room could be if you had the time and the budget to design it. Well now you do, sort of.

You and two partners are to take a room in your environment and redesign it, but you have some limitations. First, you only have $2,000 to spend. Second, you can only spend that money in one of the following stores:

An auto parts store
An art supply store
A hardware store
An office supply store
A sporting goods store

You must pick only one of these stores to spend your money in. You can use whatever items are currently in the room if you like as well. You have unlimited access to tools, so if you need to modify anything you buy or have, you can do that. You don't actually have to know how, just know it can be done. Design away!

I Should Have Picked a Speed Metal Song

Face it, some songs are just depressing. It may be their mood or the pace of the song or even the lyrics, but something about them makes you want to curl up in the bathtub and wait for morning. Music has the power to change people's moods, alter their perceptions of the world and change minds. That's pretty powerful stuff.

Visual art can do that as well. Ever stood in front of a painting and had something about it speak to you? If you haven't, you need to take tomorrow off and head down to the local art gallery and spend some time listening with your eyes. Like music, visual art has the power to affect us like few other things can.

Now, when we combine sensory input and put visual art with music, we're on to something. That's going to be our task today. Pair up into two-person teams. One person is "the music," the other is "the visual." "The music" people are charged with each picking a song that moves them, something that affects their mood, good or bad, joyful or sorrowful. The song should have the power to change your outlook when you listen to it. When you've chosen a song, give it to "the visual." That person's job is to take that song, grab a digital camera, and photograph at least ten pictures of what that song looks like. Head out into your community and look for images you can shoot that visually do what the music audibly does. If the song is slow and sorrowful, find images to shoot that match. If the song is fast and loud, find images that speak to that. It's more than just the lyrics, although those can have an influence; it has to do with the pace and mood of the song.

Swapping responsibilities can be done simultaneously, so both participants are doing both parts of the task at the same time. Both would pick a song on their own, both would exchange them, and both would shoot images that accompany their respective songs.

127

Well, It's...Um...Well, You See, He's Ummm...

Captions to images help a lot, especially when the image is a bit vague. Given enough time, we're sure you could figure out most pictures, but there is the occasional image that, simply put, is unexplainable. As simple as it may seem, that will be your task today.

Grab a partner. The two of you will be setting up and capturing three pictures that can't be explained. These shots need to be something that, without a caption, have no meaning, but with a caption, still have no meaning. Like a guy in a tux holding a blender in front of a delivery truck that overturned into a river. How do you explain that? The answer is you can't. Create three images that can't be explained.

50-50 on Whether I Should Stay or Go

"Boyshapedbox" is the Flickr screen name for Richard Krolewicz. Richard started a Flickr photostream based on a great merging of two familiar mediums: song lyrics and business charts. Here's Richard's story:

"I found this song chart for a song called 'Milkshake' by Kelis, and I posted it to my live journal. I had seen a website where someone had taken gangster rap songs and graphed and charted them but never anything other than rap, and nothing that invited others to contribute. So I posted this random chart and it got such a response that other people joined in and made one, and posted it to their blogs. Within twenty-four hours, I had collected over a hundred charts, and they just kept coming. People *loved* making them, finding them and trying to figure out what song the chart or graph represented. With all the online tools, as well as text software, it was easy to do, and very creative. I collected as many as I could find and made a Flickr group called 'Song Chart' for others to add theirs to. It was an instant hit."

4 PERSON EXERCISE

If you haven't seen the concept in action, head over to Richard's Flickr photostream immediately and take a look, because the concept is today's exercise:

www.flickr.com/photos/boyshapedbox/sets/72157603957925616

As a group, come up with a song to chart. Once you've decided on a song, each of you will separately create a song chart from a part of the song. Reassemble to share your song charts and upload them to Richard's photostream.

We Would Like to Thank the Academy...

Becoming famous and being on TV sounds like a lot of fun, but it's way more work than most would think. You have to deal with the reporters and the groupies and all that money and fame. It's obviously torture. But still, most of us are still waiting for our fifteen minutes by going to our trailer and pining for makeup. Until now, that is, when your fifteen minutes begins.

Break up into two-person teams. You will need a large box or piece of cardboard that you will decorate or design to look like the front of a TV, with a very large hole cut out for the screen. It will also help to have a video camera to record the action for posterity.

Each team is to create a series of scenes from different genres, along with a few commercial scenes. The idea is each of the teams will be acting out these scenes behind the TV, showing through the screen as if they are on TV. The scenes can and should be short, and someone should act as the remote to switch channels and give the actors the necessary cues to go to the next show or commercial. Have some fun with it, and tell your agent to get the contract signed pronto!

It's a Blender Giraffe

We all know people who are "take it apart" people. They love the opportunity to take something apart to see how it works. Typically, these people are far more interested in disassembling it than reassembling it, so there are buckets full of clock radio and CD drive parts all around the garage. While the curious will always learn from the act of taking one thing and making it many things, there's also those curious folks who see the many things as an pportunity to make something new. Creation is a powerful, intoxicating act. We're going to get a little tipsy today.

You'll need a partner for this exercise. Preferably, one of you has access to a common kitchen appliance, like a blender or a mixer, that no one is going to miss. Your task, as a team, is to take that appliance apart, piece by piece. Once that item is apart and the pieces are laid out in front of you, you are going to reassemble those parts into an animal. What kind of animal is entirely up to you two. You might need more parts, but you don't have to use all the parts of the original appliance. And don't be afraid to use a little glue in your new animal sculpture. Use whatever you need to create from what was destroyed.

Interview With

ERIC CHIMENTI

CHAPMAN UNIVERSITY
GRAPHIC DESIGN PROGRAM

There are leaders of creative teams all over the world who have the task of uniting a group of creative individuals for a common purpose or goal. They have to merge individual creative processes, join different people with different perspectives and different experiences, mold styles and talents and interests and skills into one cohesive unit for the cause of generating ideas that solve a singular problem. They are the fire-starters, the inspirers and the vision-holders. But they are also the time-managers, the whip-crackers and the idea-squashers. It's their desire and ability to succeed at wearing both the white hat and the black that makes them leaders. In their environments, they have to wear both equally well for the team to succeed.

Welcome to the familiar role of the teacher.

How strangely similar their job is to a creative director. Design programs around the world are led by people who are charged with a task traditionally assigned to the creative director of a firm or agency. Instead of conference rooms, they have classes. Instead of teams made up of professionals, they have groups made up of students. But the task is exactly the same: solve a creative problem. In this way, the design professor and the creative director are the same. They maneuver and coax, direct and coach, all with an eye on educating creative technique and inspiring creative thought.

One of these brave souls is Eric Chimenti, graphic design professor and art department chair at Chapman University in Orange, California. Eric has been teaching design for more than ten years, and in that time, he has found that teaching the technique of design is only one part of molding a creative. **You have to teach them that each project is an opportunity to find a creative solution, but most of all, you have to show them that you believe it, too.** "You have to practice what you preach," Eric starts. "The more you dig, the more you research, the more you see and experience and feed your head, the more you can bring to your students and your own design. *The students have to be shown that every project can have some aspect that inspires them, even if the whole does not. You have to show them how to find that inspiration and tap it.*"

One of the challenges that both a creative director and a design professor face is the dichotomy between creatives at different stages in their development. **While CDs have to take personalities and styles into consideration when forming project groups, design professors have to take both talent and skill into consideration when providing a creative challenge and weighing the success of the results.** Their approach inevitably plays a role in the success of the project. "In the lower-division courses," Eric reports, "we look at case studies and other assignment-appropriate, inspiring works and deconstruct what we see. In other words, we look to see how other creatives got to these solutions

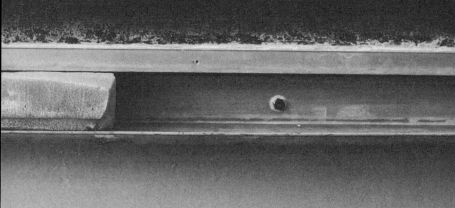

We have an open discussion of the assignment sheet and talk about what the communication problem really is, who the target audience may be, what the fictitious budget will allow and what artistic time periods may be mined for ideas that match aesthetically or ideologically. **Everybody is encouraged to share their thoughts.**

"Armed with the case study information and the classroom discussion, the students head out to do the required research for their assignment. When they return, they must have generated an overall concept statement, a mood board with ten to fifteen examples of everything from fonts to colors to textures to imagery, along with five to ten tight thumbs of what they are proposing. These are then put up on the crit wall and the students are broken into groups of three to discuss the pros and cons of what they have come up with. Only after they are done and have recorded their smaller group's feedback do they receive my feedback. This feedback is recorded and is to be reflected on and used as they move to more comprehensive solutions. They have had the benefit of a group discussion before the project began, time alone to process the information and search for appropriate solutions, time with a small group to explain and defend conceptual and aesthetic decisions, and time with a larger group looking at all the other possible approaches to the project.

"In the upper-division courses, the process is similar, but they are assigned smaller groups to work in sooner and encouraged to share research and brainstorm together even before the concept and thumbnail stage. All students also receive one-to-one help and feedback from me acting as the creative director for the project. **All students are challenged to think much more broadly at first, and then narrow and refine to a single solution.**

The younger students often don't have enough visual history and knowledge to explore everywhere they should. The older students will sometimes come up with a good solution instead of working for the best solution. So for the younger students, it is more to open their eyes and minds to the wealth of knowledge and inspiration they may not be aware of. For the older students, it is to treat them with less hand-holding, yet demand that they strive for the best over the good."

One big difference between the scholastic environment and the agency environment is the environment itself. **Agencies can mold and define their spaces to better serve the creative energy and team dynamic functionally. The scholastic environment is far more rigid and predefined.** The design professor has to address this environmental aspect and provide outlets for creative minds to experience.

"Yes," Eric admits, "This is a bit harder to do with eighteen to twenty-four people who don't all have cars, and getting out of the classroom without leaving campus means they will be distracted by other friends they see. It is solved partly by field trips that are relevant to the project, or creative games played in the classroom before, during or after the project. It is also beneficial to find some other exhibit or visual stimuli to inspire them. **As the instructor, I often bring in 'random' stuff that inspires me.** The students are also surrounded by current and past issues of design magazines, along with a university library where they can feed their heads."

The similarities in the creative process between scholastic and agency environments are easy to see. How design professors approach the classroom environment is quite similar to how a creative director approaches the team dynamic. Only the measure of success is different. And the agency cafeteria isn't open until seven.

139

Look! I'm Riding a Giant Highlighter!

A Byzantine Empire relief, dating back to 500 A.D., depicts the first known appearance of a modern-day amusement park staple: the carousel. Nowadays, mountable representations of horses, rabbits, deer and the like are adorned with colorful regalia and spin to carnival-type music the world over.

As adults, these objects offer slightly less whimsy than they did when we were children. Unless we developed some carousel subjects of our own to ride! That is your task today.

In four-person teams, develop a theme for your carousel, then each of you design your own carousel ride within your theme. You can draw them out, digitally create them or simply write the description of your ride.

2
PERSON
EXERCISE

George Washington Is Now George Clinton

In the cartoon "Daffy Doodles," Daffy Duck is the notorious "mustache fiend," drawing mustaches on every face in the city, while Porky Pig is the policeman in charge of catching him. No one wants to see mustaches drawn on faces; it's diabolical!

Drawing mustaches on printed faces is nothing new. It's a rite of passage as a youth, and sometimes as an adult. Who hasn't "defaced" the occasional headshot? (C'mon, admit it...we already know.) But there's so much more that can be done. Why stop at a mustache, especially when the subject in question is shown in a profile view? What would you do then? What would you do to, say, one of our founding fathers' profiles on a coin?

Get one other participant for this exercise. You'll need a handful of coins, preferably silver ones, as well as something to get colorful with—permanent markers, paint, you name it. The task is to use the profiles on your average coins as canvases. Add whatever magic you feel like. From hats and glasses to wigs and bandanas, it's up to you. Just be careful...Porky may slap the cuffs on you!

Pirates Don't Smell Good...

A haiku is a form of Japanese poetry that uses three lines in a 5-7-5 syllable format. It doesn't have to rhyme, it just has to stay to the syllable structure. You can write a haiku about anything, which we're going to prove today.

3 PERSON EXERCISE

You'll need two other participants for this exercise. The rules of this exercise are simple:

All write one haiku,
Each person writing one line,
Until it's complete.

Don't coach each other on what to write, simply write your line and pass it to the next person. There's one more restriction, though. You have to write the haiku about one of these themes:

Bad habits of the group
Pirate problems
Bowling gets a bad rap
Dentistry is fun
The printer is not a friend
Home tattoos never work
Waiting in line
Macs versus PCs

Write one haiku for each of these topics, switching the order in which each person writes a line.

The Sixty-Four-Ounce Cup of Coffee Gave You Away

On New Year's Eve 2007, a woman got in a taxi in New York City to find a very nice digital camera. The taxi driver had no interest in finding the owner of the camera, so the woman took it home and decided to find the owner herself. Unfortunately, all she had were the photos on the camera to solve the mystery. By deciphering information found within the photos, the woman was able to locate the owner of the camera, half a world away in Australia.

While we may not have three hundred vacation photos to use as clues, there's something to taking what little information we are given and deciphering the solution. That's what we're going to do today.

This exercise is for any size group, but groups of eight to twelve would be ideal. Everyone will need a digital camera. **Take ten to fifteen photos of your normal routine for an entire day, keeping yourself out of the shots.** Take the photos off of the camera and burn them to a nondescript CD. The next day, find a way to randomly exchange CDs so no one knows which CD belongs to whom. Your task is to figure out whose CD you have, with only the pictures on the CD as clues. Good luck!

Mom, Can Billy and I Get Bunk Desks for Work? Please?

As more and more people get hired at your organization, space is getting tighter and tighter. It's not uncommon for people to share spaces, with two people per uninspiring cubicle. It's bad enough you are burdened with three-and-a-half gray-carpet-lined walls; now you have to share that space with someone else. Something needs to be done, and you two are just the team to do it!

You two have been given an unlimited amount of resources (possible), unlimited support (not out of the realm of possibility), and an unlimited budget (not a chance). Your task is to redesign the cubicle to fit two people. The restrictions of the space are evident: You can't move the walls. Everything else is fair game. How would you design the common cubicle to fit two people comfortably, and how would you modify (read: trick out) the cubicle if your unlimited budget and resources were, indeed, a fact and not a strange fantasy you imagined after a few too many umbrella-clad refreshments?

Spatulas! Start Your Engines!

Most agencies and firms have some form of kitchen or lunch-room area. These areas typically offer the bare necessities for lunchtime activities, like a microwave, refrigerator and a host of utensils, plates, cups and the like. That's a good thing, because without those staples of culinary interest, you wouldn't be able to build and race your car.

Um...what?!

Don't tell me you've never built a pinewood-derby-style car primarily out of objects commonly found in most kitchens. That's absurd! How did you earn your "Creative Human" card without such experience? Well, we don't have much time then. You've got to create your cars and race them before the Creativity Police come a-knockin' on your door, if you know what I mean.

You're going to need someone (or multiple someones) to race. A one-car race is just sad, so find at least one other card-deprived creative and let's build your cars! First, you're going to need one thing not commonly found in the kitchen: wheels and axles. These can be found at just about any hobby store for cheap. Once you have wheels and axles for your car, head to the kitchen for the rest.

You can use whatever you find in the kitchen as your car body. You can assemble, glue, paint and construct whatever you find there to create your car. The only restriction is that you need to be able to attach your wheels and axles to the body for race time.

Once you've constructed your cars, you're going to need a flat, downhill surface to race. Ramps are good; stairs are bad. Get racing!

I'd Like to Thank Erica in Client Services for Giving Me My First Shot

Only the best of the best get elected into their respective hall of fame. Good doesn't cut it; it takes great to be enshrined within those hallowed halls. The greatest achievements, the greatest performers, the greatest leaders. It's the ultimate award, the culmination of a lifetime of dedication and sacrifice. The bond shared between those select few lasts a lifetime.

But what about you?

You deserve to be in a hall of fame, right? You've sacrificed. You're dedicated, most of the time. You have great achievements and amazing performances. You deserve to be enshrined right along side of the greats...of your office environment. (You didn't think we were suggesting Cooperstown or anything, did you?) Not only do you deserve induction into your hall of fame, since there isn't a hall of fame yet, you, along with two of your fellow initial inductees, deserve to create it. The three of you are going to create your workplace's hall of fame, what requirements are needed for induction, what kind of induction ceremony is planned and who are the inaugural inductees (which include you, of course). Just make sure the bronze bust features your good side.

The Ump's a Bum, but My Seat Warmer Is Nice

If you've ever sat in the bleacher seats at a professional baseball game, you know the sorry state of your derrière shortly after. The bleachers are hard and uncomfortable, and they support the craziest, rowdiest, most dedicated fans a team could ever have. The bleachers are the cheap seats, and as such are the targets of the hard-lined faithful who attend almost every home game of an incredibly long season. These tried-and-true fans deserve more. Move them to the front row? Not a chance. The front row isn't good enough for these fans. They deserve more. Professional baseball teams pay out close to $100 million to their players. It's time to give some back to the bleacher bums.

Grab one other participant for this exercise. Your task today is to collaborate and develop the ideal bleacher improvements. Take into account who the average bleacher bums are and what they could use. Money and technology are no object. Design the ideal bleacher experience. They deserve it. Let's play two!

Get Your Game Face On—
It's Pencil-Jousting Time

In offices big and small, all across this great nation, two brave souls face battle. Armed and prepared, they stare down one another with fierce competitive drive. Grunting and frothing at the mouths, the combatants prepare to play the blood sport of kings: Faceball. Wha? What's that? **YOU'VE NEVER HEARD OF FACEBALL?!** Are you a hermit? Go here and catch up: **www.faceball.org**.

Good to have you back. Faceball was the brainchild of Flickr's John Allspaw and Dunstan Orchard. It's a terribly dramatic game where combatants sit across from one another in competitive saddles called "chairs" and hurl beach balls at each other's faces. What's that, you say? It's a silly game? Heresy! Let's see you invent something better.

Grab another competitor for this exercise. Your task today is to create an office game that is sure to become corporate lore and the stories told to your children and your children's children. You have to be able to keep score because, like all things worthy of such glory, there must be a pathetic, whimpering loser.

We're On a Mission...
From the Production Manager

You and three partners are a mega-super band, put together to make millions, save babies and rock the world! No one will be able to darken your awesomeness. Groupies will flock, roadies will move stuff a lot, and after-parties will last three-and-a-half days. Some have even speculated that your assembly was divine and predicted by prophets, although no proof has ever been documented.

4
PERSON EXERCISE

Now that we've established who you are as a group, it's time to establish who you are as individuals. Decide as a group what instruments or roles each of you play in the group. You then need to individually write your own bios and histories. Discuss your backgrounds, both musical and human, what musical influences you have, maybe a quote or two. **You are a rock god**—write like one! Come back together to discuss your bios and name your band. Tour stops in accounting are optional.

4

**PERSON
EXERCISE**

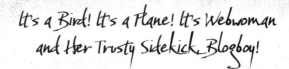

It's a Bird! It's a Plane! It's Webwoman and Her Trusty Sidekick, Blogboy!

You are [insert your name here]. At least, that's who you want people to think you are. You see, [insert your name here] is just a cover; it's a mask for your secret identity. You have a secret you've been hiding, and it has nothing to do with that spring break in college. You are a superhero, aren't you? You have superpowers that no one knows about—at least, no one who knows you as [insert your name here]. You and three partners all have secret powers. You all change into your superhero costumes and fight crime in the name of all that is lawful and good.

At least, you will when you get done with this exercise.

The four of you are going to document your superhero-ness, but you're going to do it for someone in the group other than yourself. First, randomly exchange names so that every person in the group gets the name of a different person, but don't let anyone know who you have. Next, write out what you see as that person's superhero name, where he came from, his superpowers and how he came to have them. If you're feeling especially spicy, draw out his superhero outfit. When everyone is done, reveal the superhero behind the mild-mannered persona.

Nick Promised Fresh
Bagels if I Chose Him

Billboard advertising is about punch.

What can be said that resonates with consumers who are whizzing by at 70 miles per hour? It has to be short, quick, powerful and memorable. The message has to convince people to act...when they get to their destinations. That better be a pretty memorable message! In theory, the philosophy wouldn't change even if the size of the billboard and the speed of the travelers did. Let's test that theory today.

You need another willing participant for this exercise. Advertising is competition, so it's time to test competing messages and see who has the goods to incite people to action. The two of you are going to create competing billboards and see whose message encourages more action. First, you're going to need to construct real billboards, just at much smaller scales. You'll want to create the billboards to accommodate the available standard size of your color printer. If you have a printer that can accommodate an 11" x 17" sheet, then make your billboard fit that size. If you don't, make your billboard fit whatever maximum size you can print in color.

Next, you'll need to construct the actual billboards. If you have tabletop surfaces, you'll need to build a stand of some form. If you have wall space you're going to use, you'll need to build a frame that can be hung.

When you've built your billboard stand or frame, it's time to get down to business. You'll need a measurable commodity to decide who the most effective marketer is. This can be encouraging people to give to a charity or a party fund, or to choose your bowl of M&M's over your competition's bowl. Decide on some measurable goal.

Now it's time for the message. Develop your campaign however you see fit. You can change your message as often as you like. It doesn't have to be designed if that's not your cup of tea; you could develop a campaign of words or even drawings. Whatever will incite walkers whizzing by at 70 steps per minute to consider your product or service over your competition. Placement will play a role as well. You can choose to place your billboard wherever you like, changing its location however you see fit. Find a high-traffic area in your office or agency and advertise your way to victory!

I Call It Stock Car Boxing

In 1998, director David Zucker released a movie about a game he had invented years earlier, BASEketball. A combination of basketball and baseball, BASEketball combines the common HORSE shooting game with a baseball scoring system. The game sparks an interesting question: Can other sports be combined in a similar manner? You're going to find out today.

You'll need one other sports-minded participant for this exercise. You are going to combine two sports to make two new ones. First, each of you should choose a sport you know and love. Reveal your sports to one another. The goal is to base your new sport on your original sport with your partner's sport mixed in, and your partner will do the same.

For instance, if you chose football and your partner chose hockey, you would have to create a new sport with football as the base and adding elements of hockey into it, while your partner would be starting with hockey as the base and adding elements of football into the game.

When you're done creating your new game, call up David Zucker and see if he's busy directing anything at the moment. You never know!

I'll Trade You Three Junior Account Execs for Your Rookie Web Developer

You've waited your whole life for this moment. All those sweat-drenched days training. All those exercises. All the fonts you've looked through. All the Pantone books you've pored over. They all have led to this moment, the day you'll finally get that one item that makes all the hard work worth it, the thing that will announce to the world that you've arrived: your rookie card. This is the first, the one people will collect for years to come. You'll be right there along with the superstars. You're a pro. And you deserve a trading card.

That's the task for you and your team today. You are going to be making trading cards of one another. First, take the names of everyone in your team and draw them out of a hat so you receive the name of someone other than yourself. Your task is to create the trading card for this person. It can start with a photograph and you can draw around the photograph, you can do it digitally or you can just sketch it out. Your task is to take who the person is and what he or she does and make a trading card out of it.

You'll also need to create the back of the card, with the person's career stats, background info and highlights. Make it all up, or get pieces of real information if you like. When you're all done, let the trading begin! How many rookie production assistants are worth one creative director?

4 PERSON EXERCISE

interview with

JOHN JANUARY

Sullivan, Higdon and Sink

If you fire up your computer and go to **www.wehatesheep.com**, you might think you were about to experience the wonderful world of mattress manufacturing, or perhaps you'd be dropped into the blog of anti-livestock zealots, or maybe the doorway to a society against wool. What you wouldn't expect, though, is to be presented with the passionate philosophy of a Kansas City ad agency. Why would an ad agency hate sheep? They're so cute and fluffy! "They remind us of the type of marketing that follows instead of leads," quips John January, Sullivan Higdon & Sink's executive creative director. John has been hating sheep at SHS for almost two decades, touting the virtues of Borderless Branding for clients like Pizza Hut, American Century Investments and Westar Energy.

John's passionate pursuit of the idea has taught him many things over the years, none more true than the power of **collaborative creativity**. Back before today's "innovative" shops were "re-engineering" away from the traditional "writer/ art director" model, John and his management team at SHS had already abolished all departments in lieu of an integrated team structure. They've had the last twelve years to perfect a model that sees a client team of art directors and account supervisors, client relation directors and writers, production artists and accountants putting aside personal ego for the chance to create the big idea.

"We have a saying," John begins. "'**Let the idea have the ego.**' That means those who traditionally see themselves as the idea-makers are being joined in that task by those who traditionally have been pushed aside during idea generation. We've evolved this model to not only see what works with collaborative creativity, but to specifically hire for it. Many creatives simply aren't built for that type of collaboration. Group ownership of ideas is so different than what designers grow up knowing. **The integration of the team means we have to find creatives that aren't just willing to buy into the model, they're programmed for it—they naturally work together and look at the big idea first and their role second.**

"There will never come a time when people who think creatively, tell stories and find insight within data aren't valuable. Creatives are not going to lose their place. The value of creativity is higher than ever. It's just that we're looking to express it in so many new ways and through so many new channels that the traditional advertising model of writer/art director isn't the most effective way to work anymore."

So how does this collaborative method work with so many roles playing equal parts in the process? "People are still ultimately responsible form their own discipline," John imparts, "in the sense that art directors design, writers write, etc. But the input from other types of people is critical. In the shared, collaborative environment, there are two keys to success. The first one is **trust**. You have to trust the people in your team are going to hit it out of the park. There is a lot of vulnerability in the creative process. The safety net within the traditional art director/writer team is the seclusion of the team, ideas are just coming from the two, all the ugly ideas get hidden and only the good ones see the light of day. In the collaborative model, you have to develop that bond and that trust in a wider group, be willing to fail and share ideas before they've had a chance to be refined. As a leader, you have to foster that trust.

"The second key to succeeding with this model is **chemistry**. In the traditional model, many times, you had pairings that just didn't work. The creative chemistry just wasn't there. This is true of larger, more collaborative groups as well. Success often hinges on the leader's ability to play creative matchmaker. Putting together team members who may seem like odd choices based on their responsibilities may seem like right groupings based on what their strengths and perspectives are. Chemistry matters, so leaders should look for the people who have that creative connection, regardless of responsibility."

One of the by-products of a collaborative environment is the organic process of group ideation. As teams get more inclusive, the chance for impromptu gatherings and idea-sharing sessions increases. John reports, "In our office, the walls are whiteboards. Each team has a series or set of ever-expanding whiteboards that let teams contribute and let ideas grow. Initial brainstorming meetings usually involve a lot

163

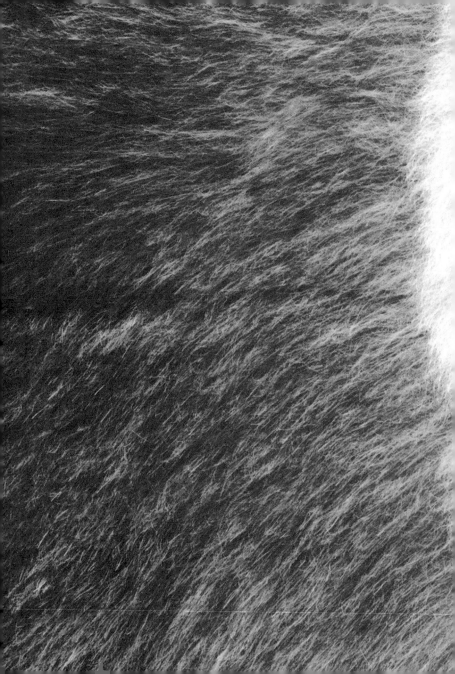

of unplanned sketching and writing on the walls, then as we break up, we find smaller groups organically begin to form to further ideas that have been offered. These smaller groups are often made up of varying job titles, where people start to gather with other smaller groups to share and grow ideas. We set up loosely based structures of milestones, but what happens in between is the organic nature of a collaborative creative process.

"It's amazing what happens when you do away with departmental politics. With truly shared success, everyone is focused on doing great work for the client and isn't worried about their own role in that idea. You find it very easy to share people, talent and resources with other teams because the people coming into your team, regardless of their purpose, aren't a threat—they're allies brought in to help create and nurture ideas."

To John, leading a team isn't about the ego, it's about the process. If given the chance to offer one piece of advice to a newly appointed team leader, he would put it this way:

"It's not about you. It's about the idea."

And it's clearly not about sheep.

Vote Ramon for King, He Promises to Give You All an Extra Day Off

Getting elected to office is an arduous task, full of campaign trails, issue debates, kissing babies and shaking hands. Nominees promise everything they can, skirt difficult issues and generally market themselves as the perfect candidate for the job. It isn't always the candidate with the best credentials who wins; often, it's the candidate with the best marketing who wins. *You're going to explore that dynamic in today's task.*

You'll need a willing partner for this exercise. The task is for both of you to run for office in your environment. Most likely, you won't be able to campaign for your boss' job, although that would be a comical development. Instead, you'll be campaigning for a position much more worthy of adoration: king or queen of your environment. Your goal is to convince the voting population to elect you king or queen. You'll need to ramp up the marketing machine to accomplish your goal, so you'll need a platform to stand on (not a literal platform, that would be silly, a political platform ... a group of beliefs you are standing for). You'll need campaign buttons, marketing slogans, a list of promises you have no intention of keeping and some babies to kiss.

You'll also need to set up the voting system, when the vote takes place, and what the loser has to be subjected to in humiliating defeat.

Thou Shalt Bring Blueberry Bagels to Work Every Monday

In the book of Exodus, God gave Moses two stone tablets that listed God's commandments for his followers to abide by. Mel Brooks would argue it was fifteen commandments and Moses dropped one of the tablets, but that's another story. Regardless, commandments are meant to be empirical laws that must be followed. In your environment, such laws need to be created to ensure harmony, and you're just the person to bring them back from Mount Sinai...er...the copier.

Find two other willing participants for this exercise. The three of you will be creating your environment's ten commandments, give or take a few. Collaborate to create the laws all should follow, whether they are "Thou shalt" or "Thou shalt not." If one of them is "Thou shalt not participate in any creative exercises," please move on to the next exercise and forget you ever saw this one.

PERSON EXERCISE

... Unless the Muffins Are Fresher

Now that you've created your environment's ten commandments, these hard-lined, can't-be-broken rules, it's time to break them. **What good are rules if there aren't exceptions to the rules?**

The three of you will collaborate to come up with the ten exceptions to the rules, one exception per commandment. This will give you an out to that "Thou shalt not be late to production meetings" one.

And If You Shant, May the Fleas of a Thousand Camels Infest Your Armpits

Now that you've developed your ten commandments and your ten exceptions, it's time to dictate what the punishment is for breaking the commandments. In this day and age, with all the input we have, it's too easy to ask you to come up with ten horrifying punishments for breaking the commandments. Frankly, we're afraid of what you'd come up with. No, there is a restriction to this exercise. You have to write what the punishments would be as if you lived in these five eras in time:

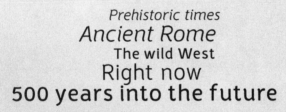

Prehistoric times
Ancient Rome
The wild West
Right now
500 years into the future

The three of you are each to write one punishment for each historical time, in the language and brutality of the time. Make the punishments fit the crime, or go for the jugular (pun intended) and make sure no one ever breaks the commandments!

The Postal Service: Because Getting Your Package Undamaged Is for Wusses

We've all seen our share of bad advertising headlines. Usually when we say "bad," we mean "ineffective." There are few headlines out there that are truly "bad." Probably because to be horrendous would mean to communicate a point or feature that is contrary to the product or service being advertised, and even the most harebrained of dimwits can tell if a headline is damaging the purpose of the ad. Or can they?

Grab another willing advertising guru to help with this exercise. You are going to take your average, pedestrian service and you're going to write headlines for it that are atrocious. Say, for instance, you were doing an ad for the U.S. Postal Service. Your task is to collaborate and write up ten terrible headlines for the U.S. Postal Service, headlines no postal service on Earth would run. But there's a twist: The headlines all have to be true, to some extent. They can be a stretch, but at their core, they can't be out-and-out fabrications. Truth in advertising, you know!

I See You Blew Up Your Balloon. It's a Hot Air Balloon, Then?

4 PERSON EXERCISE

At the turn of the 20th century, the first successful transatlantic hot air balloon voyage occurred. Since then, folks have been flying hot air balloons across oceans and over mountains. Many festivals still exist today to fly these gargantuan creatures and even race the balloons. We're going to pay homage to these hot air balloon racers today with some balloon races of our own.

You will need at least four total competitors and a bag of large-size balloons for today's activity. Each of you is going to create your own racing balloon. You can decorate the balloon however you see fit. Your balloon must, however, carry a basket of some form. Make a basket out of paper and secure it to the bottom of the balloon with string and tape. When you have created your balloon, you'll need to secure an elevated position and a target or goal. Hanging out of an upper-floor window or on top of the roof of a building would work. Set up a target below and let the balloons float down in a race for the ages. The closest one to the target wins.

The Fragile, Sweet Rose Drifted Lightly in the Breeze; Then an Elephant Came, and...

There's a tried-and-true creative writing exercise that encourages stuck writers to break out of their funk by taking a random spot in the story and inserting two characters that walk into the room with guns. The idea behind the abrupt insertion of gunmen into the story is to force action by requiring the characters on the story to react to the situation. We're going to take that same concept, but we're going to amp it up by forcing action into a four-person chain story.

PERSON EXERCISE

You'll need three other storytellers for this exercise. The four of you will be chain writing a story, which means one person starts with an opening sentence, then passes the story to the next person, who writes the next line of the story and passes it to the third person, who does the same. The fourth person's job is to force action by inserting a random, aggressive act. Start with "Two men with guns enter the room" but each subsequent time, create a new aggressive act to insert into the story and pass it on. The other three storytellers must react to the aggressive turn and continue writing. Keep going for at least three rotations through the order, and on the fourth, end the story. What you should have is quite possibly the most twisted tale known to man, and a Cannes Film Festival screenplay.

And Then Johnny Ate a Desk Lamp and Kicked a Rutabaga

Everyone thinks they can write a children's book, but communicating as quickly and effectively as a children's book author has to—with as few words and pictures as the books have—is much harder than it seems. The length of that last sentence alone represents the size of the whole story in most children's books. Just because the language is simple doesn't make the job any easier. In many ways, it makes it more challenging. Some children's books don't have words at all—they communicate a whole story entirely in pictures. That's a tall order, but it's one you thankfully won't have to take today.

Your task is to create a children's book about your occupation or industry. Grab another willing participant for this exercise. The two of you will be splitting up the job of writing and illustrating. Now, don't get all bent out of shape over the word "illustrating." It just means one of you will be in charge of the pictures, and the other, the words.

First, create a book by taking three sheets of copy paper as a group and folding them in half to create a twelve-page booklet, and staple it in the crease. Now, the person who will be providing the pictures can do it in a number of ways. On the right side of every spread, you can draw simple scenes, you can find imagery on the Internet to print and glue, you could create a collage of found imagery...anything you want to create the images. They shouldn't be created to a story, though; they should be random images. After the illustrator has filled every right-side page with images, the writer's task is to take the book of random images and build a children's story by weaving the images, page by page, into a tale. Use the left side of every spread to write that spread's part in the story. It can be as long or short as you want.

When the story is finished, collaborate to name your story and create the cover. If it's still appropriate for children, read it to a group of kids and find out if your story scares or cares!

My Story Is Called "The Flying Red Asparagus"

Writing a story isn't about having all the pieces ahead of time. Often, a great short story starts with almost nothing and evolves over time to be something wonderful. Creativity works the exact same way. An idea might not be completely fleshed out at the beginning, but offering that idea up to be taken by others and evolve over time will grow that idea into the most it can be. We're going to explore the idea of the evolving short story for today's exercise.

You'll need two other storywriters for today's exercise. Each of you is to come up with a random word. It can be a noun, an adjective or a verb, it's your choice. When everyone has a word, write all three on a piece of paper. Each of you will write a short story connecting those three words. It can be a paragraph or a page, whatever you need to connect the words or the ideas of the words into a short story. When you're done, read the stories aloud and see how different perspectives can create different takes on the same elements.

Pizza by Day, Runway Model by Night

In the last exercise, you wrote a story based on three random words that you connected together. Let's take the concept one step further. Each of the three participants should thumb through a magazine and find a random photo. Once each of you has found a photo, lay them on the table in a line a few inches apart. Instead of taking three random words and connecting them through a story, write a short story that connects these three images together. You can simply develop a story that incorporates the three images in some way, or you can take it up a notch by writing a story that connects these three images in order, as you see them on the table. In essence, you're writing what is between the pictures—the story that occurs in the spaces.

The Smell of Pinocchio's Shorts Is Overpowering My Porridge

There's nothing like that new car smell, huh? It's such a desirable smell that inventive air freshener companies have captured it and encourage you to hang that new car smell from your rearview mirror, even if that mirror is attached to a '79 Gremlin. There are other recognizable smells that would make good air fresheners, like the leather straps from a guillotine, torch oil or freshly polished armor. Well, those might be the air fresheners of choice if you lived in medieval times. Which is exactly the type of thinking you're going to need for this next exercise.

You'll need three other fresh-smelling participants for this exercise. The four of you will be creating a set of rearview mirror-hanging air fresheners for the following five themes:

A children's storybook land

The Oval Office

Your environment

The 1960s

The wild West

Each of you is to create one air freshener scent for each theme. Together, you will have a four-scent pack for each theme, and a new marketing angle to make a little dough on the side.

Spacious 100-Square-Foot Cubicle With Cozy Breakfast Nook

Thumbing through real estate publications, the agents who write up the listings should change occupations and write political speeches. They are so incredibly clever with the way they describe houses, personifying a property until you almost feel like you've visited it.

We're going to visit that world a little today. Grab a willing participant for this exercise. The two of you will be writing a real estate-style listing for each other's work area. Take a moment to visit your partner's primary work area. If you'd like, take a couple pictures of some of the "features" you'll be selling in the listing. Now, write up the listing as if your partner's work area was a property for sale. Expound on the features in paragraph form, as well as listing out the specs for the space. When it's all done, start entertaining offers and see if you can't make a little on the side.

The Theme Is Themeless—Good Luck

Veer provides visual elements for use in professional creative work—such as graphic design, motion design, advertising and filmmaking—including stock photography, illustration, typefaces, and unique merchandise and services. One of those services is an area of the Veer website called "Ideas," where they provide various forms of creative entertainment and information. Within this section is a contest that Veer calls "Lightboxing," where they pit two graphic designers against one another by providing five images from their stock photography library in a digital lightbox, and assigning a general theme like "Midnight" or "Mad scientist." The designers are to take those five images and assemble together a single image that speaks to the theme. Users vote on the creations, and a winner is crowned.

We're going to perform a similar exercise today. This exercise requires a knowledge of photo-editing software, like Adobe Photoshop. First, you'll need two combatants. Next, have an unbiased third party choose a theme and five images from a stock photography website like Veer that are loosely tied to that theme and place them into a digital lightbox. The two contestants can use any combination of the five images to create a piece of art that satisfies the theme. Just stay away from themes like "Bosses suck."

With Plastic Clothes, Stains Don't Stand a Chance

A full-page ad in a magazine is a lot of real estate to use when you're designing. But a spread, where you have two pages side by side to use, is like a parking lot in comparison. With all that space, you have the room to use one full page on just the image, and one full page on the headline, the product, the logo and all the body copy you need to convince readers to buy your product.

Often, the image that is displayed on one side of the ad's spread is self-explanatory. Other times, it has no meaning without the accompanying page. We're going to explore the latter in today's exercise.

Grab another willing participant for this exercise. The two of you will be teaming up to create a spread ad, with one of you taking the image side, and the other taking the payoff side. The partner who has the image side is to go through a magazine and find a full-page image that has no text or product identification of any kind. You are looking for an image that needs the payoff side of the spread ad to explain the concept, so your image should be random and clean (both partners should be finding an image so you can each do the exercise from both perspectives).

When you both have found your image, exchange images. You now need to add the "payoff" side of the spread ad. Using the image you have, you need to create what the ad is for by creating a headline, a product and any body copy you feel is necessary to communicate the concept. Either create the spreads digitally or simply paste the image to the left side of an 11" x 17" piece of paper and sketch, write or glue cutouts on the right side.

3
PERSON EXERCISE

I Call the Media Room Next to the Air Duct

How many of you had a tree house when you were young? How many still have one? How many want to rent it out as a loft apartment to make a couple extra bucks? We hear ya. Tree houses are kids' sanctuaries, the place they go to play and dream and get away. Sounds like something all of us would want, huh? It's time we get it.

You'll need two other participants for this exercise. The three of you will be evaluating your space and planning where you're going to put your inner-office tree house. The restrictions are that it has to be within your office environment, it has to be off the ground and it has to be the awesomest, most wickedest, coolest tree house, like, ever! Collaborate to sketch out its size and scale, what it looks like from the exterior. Then, take the unlimited budget your boss just gave you (it can happen!) and write out what it would have inside it. The sky's literally the limit. You'll also need to decide who's in the club and, therefore, who can use the tree house.

I Hope You Have a Crappy Day and You Get Fired or Something

In 1910, a slender eighteen-year-old named Joyce Clyde Hall hopped off a train in Kansas City, Missouri, with a box of picture postcards under his arm. Joyce Clyde Hall started selling these picture postcards, and the empire that is known as Hallmark was born.

Greeting cards provide a way of saying just about anything, such as "Happy Birthday" and "Get Well Soon." They also can become fairly twisted greetings, if the occasion is right (or wrong, depending on how you look at it). We're going for "wrong" today.

Get another twisted friend for this exercise. Each of you is to find three random images online and e-mail them to one another. These three images will constitute the outside of a series of three greeting cards each of you will be creating. The more twisted the imagery is, the more fun the exercise will be.

After you have each received your images from the other person, create the inside of the card that pays off the image on the outside. It can be for a traditional event, like a birthday or a wedding, or it can be for some made-up or alternative event. Just make sure the message on the inside of the card does justice to the image on the outside of the card. When complete, send the cards around to your twisted friends.

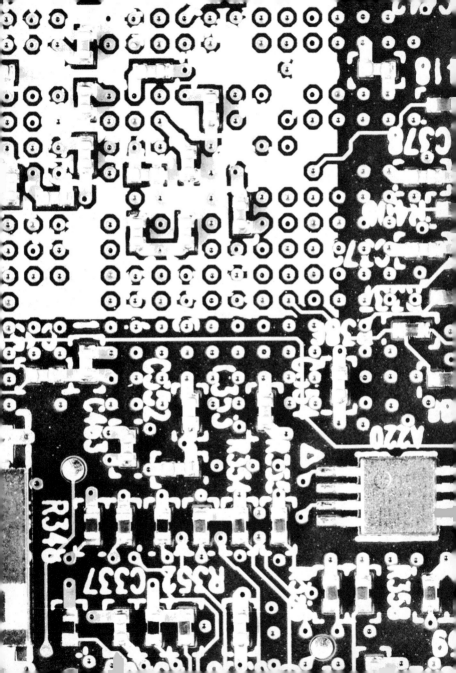

INTERVIEW WITH **THE**

HOW

FORUM

On the surface, most social forums are just the visual representation of code, but it seems like in the HOW forums, *HOW* magazine's digital gathering place for tens of thousands of creatives, there's something a little more organic below the surface. It may just seem like a techy collection of fonts and avatars, but there's a real purpose behind the text. **It's not just words, it's thoughts. It's not just cold answers, it's warm responses.** In reality, the HOW forums seem to be far more human than many flesh-and-blood creative teams. And make no mistake…this is a team.

To many "HOWies," the HOW forums are the only creative feedback they receive, human or otherwise. Many forum participants don't have agencies or firms: They have a workstation and a chair. Contrary to popular belief, the creative industry is effectively fueled by these renegade souls, stretching the accepted "norm" of the industry in valiant attempts to produce amazingly creative work, one piece at a time. To these people, the HOW forums offer constructive critiques, social equality and creative recharge around every post. They are a team, and they're fiercely loyal to both their craft and their group. Being a part of this team, however, is relatively easy: Show up and participate.

Before understanding how a "team of individuals" can effectively work, it's crucial to understand how the faithful forum members, the lifeblood of this digital assembly, see their own collective environment. "First off," says Steve Wilson, aka SAW, "the HOW forum is chock-full of great talent, covering the gamut of design fields. So, I believe that just being around this group, whether it's talking shop or goofing off, is a wonderful creativity booster. **Just being around creatives makes me feel creative.**

"But it's also about a whole lot more. It's about sharing and viewing great work on the HOW Fridge. It's about learning new techniques, getting some cool Photoshop brushes or sharing helpful business practices. It's seeing Von Glitschka's step-by-step process in completing a masterful illustration…and the fact that he trusts us enough to share that. That's the essence of creatives helping creatives."

Michelle Underwood, aka mLu, adds, "I've learned a lot of valuable lessons through others' experiences and have made many friends just by posting and checking in regularly. As a 'newbie,' it was always (and still is) wonderful to learn from everyone's experiences and be able to ask questions without feeling like an idiot. Everyone here comes from a different walk of life, and it brings even more to the table for growth."

"I'm an in-house designer," says Nicholas J. Nawroth, aka n2, "and for a long time, I was the sole in-house designer at my company. Since joining this forum, we've added another designer. But she has been on maternity leave. So I really don't have anybody at work to discuss design with. I really enjoy coming to the forum to keep up on design trends, discuss the latest design news, goof off a bit and see what everyone else is up to. In fact, I've been exposed to more design knowledge and resources because of the HOW forum— more than I think one person can ever really absorb! I also believe seeing other designers' works really inspires me and pushes me to be a better designer."

There's a lot of talk about the ultimate HOW forums collaboration example, the *HOWiezine*, which is a handmade book project created entirely by HOWies. For the project, a theme is introduced, and anyone who wants to participate can create two pages based on his or her interpretation of that theme. HOWies create it, and the HOWies who participate in it get a copy. It's an impressive display of collaborative inspiration.

"I think a creative team could learn new things about each other and relate to each other in new ways if they got involved with the *HOWiezine*," HOW forum uber-member Patti Bachelder, aka Pad Thai, says. "It's most inspiring to me that designers from all over participate (in addition to American designers, we've had participants from Canada, the UK, France, Mexico and New Zealand) and are willing to put time and ingenuity into creating 'the sum of the parts' for people they've never met. There's a level of trust that whatever effort I put into it, others will also invest. And getting to know each other on the forum and through the

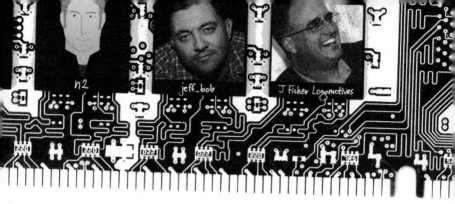

n2   jeff_bob   J Fisher Locomotives

HOWiezine has created friendships that share a sense of humor and respect for opinions about what we're doing that we thirst for, but sometimes can't get in the workplace."

"I have to agree with Pad Thai about the *HOWiezine*," Halftone Dot (whose real name shall remain anonymous) interjects. "It's a great creative exercise, probably the best one, although we've done some less-involved funny ones. They've become our own proprietary exercises, things that mean something to us as a group and keep the beach ball bouncing through threads, like Vondize the head, Pic Association game, Threadkiller thread, Creative Blender, SAW's Bar, Add to the Story threads, Solve the Puzzle threads...

All of these things make us laugh, bring some joy and help us step away from the mundane. They reenergize us."

Karma Savage, aka ksavage, adds, "I let *HOWiezine* sign-ups go by over and over before I finally fell in love with a *HOWiezine* theme: superheroes. I've been hooked ever since. I love seeing the creative pages of the HOWies. Unbelievable inspiration."

It's not all about the creative expression for these Howies. These are professional creatives, and as such, the left sides and right sides of their brains are constantly battling. **The forums provide a place to get not just creative advice, but business advice as well.**

Mary   mayhemstudios   RonMan   Ned

"Another great forum feature is the business section," adds Prax Cruz, aka PlushCadillac. "For a freelancer, that section is tremendously helpful. **I can go in there, ask a question, and know that I will be given good advice that is generally backed up by a real-world example.** And in turn, I try to give as much as I can. Just this morning, I called up a HOWie asking about something I saw on her site, and we ended up talking and exchanging ideas and stories, and I got some really good info and advice. *In the end, I can say that with the forum, I feel like I have a team of people that I can go to and count on.*"

The digital environment makes for a convenient meeting place, as proximity becomes unneeded, but there are still times when even the stoutest of digerati desires creative human interaction. In those times, this team doesn't need to look outside of their own environment; they ave a whole globe of team members to choose from.

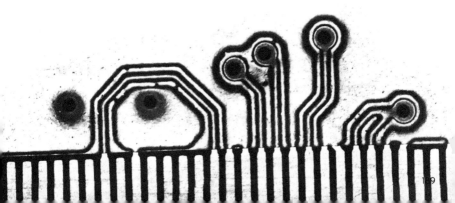

FROM LEFT TO RIGHT: Lisa, Pad Thai, LadyLuck, SAW,

Rohan, Lauren3g, n2

"I've been fortunate to live in three different places within the U.S. during my HOW forum years," ksavage writes, "and I've met some of my online friends at local meet-ups. Creatively awesome. HOWie meet-ups are a must, if possible."

"The first time I met HOWies in real life," Halftone Dot adds, "I drove ten hours to Atlanta for what we called the 'KnowHow'—a meet-up organized by Bruce and Pad Thai for those of us who couldn't make the HOW Design Conference. It was fantastic. We had sessions and swag and food and fellowship."

"That KnowHOW was really groundbreaking in a lot of ways," adds Bruce Schneider, aka BruceS63. "It's one thing to get to know one another online, but in person is another story. I think we found that everyone was pretty much who they seemed to be on the HOW forums, in a good way."

"Two of the folks I met on the forum I chat with regularly via instant message," n2 explains. "I was developing my new identity system, which consists of an illustration of me. I wanted to update my illustration of me and via IM, I worked back and forth with my HOWies to refine my illustration and identity system. These particular people have been helpful for bouncing ideas off of on freelance work as well. Right now, I'm chatting with a HOWie via IM, and I'm going to give her a lesson in Photoshop masking. Many people (myself included) start a thread called 'brainstorming' when they are stuck for ideas, and folks usually have some great material to help get the poster's creativity sparked."

While the forums provide a comfortable, accepting environment for team members, it also provides a forum (pun intended) for design critique. **When you work alone, or don't have opinions you value to look at your work and give feedback, the forums are more than happy to help.** "I was told of HOW's 'brutal' critique section and ventured over here," admits Kirsten Jackes, aka phoenix, "not to post, but to learn how to better dissect a design, why something is out of place, etc. It wasn't so much that I didn't know, but more that I couldn't articulate my thoughts. I've now been adding to the critiques, being aware of being constructive and helpful. This helps form my own ideas (I brainstorm in my head what would I do from scratch, and what would I do to help the concept shown) to understand some elements of design better and provide a different perspective."

It's clear that physical presence isn't a requirement to build a rustworthy, motivated team. If more teams of creatives who sit within feet of one another every day could have the chemistry and good-willed camaraderie of the HOWies, I think we'd see a dramatic increase in passionate creative output. And smileys.

I'm Gonna Go All S'more on You Today

Remember when Matt "borrowed" your staple remover last week and never brought it back? Or when Courtney took the last packet of ranch dressing at the team lunch? It's time they get the payback they deserve. They just earned a ticket to Mallowtown.

You'll need at least four combatants for today's battle royale. Next, you'll need to head down to your local toy shop or click over to any number of online retailers and pick yourself up some marshmallow guns. These air-powered, fluffy-ammo'd weapons hurl harmless marshmallows, both the small and big sizes, with incredible accuracy. You'll also need some ammunition, so pick up a couple bags of marshmallows at the store. The fight is on!

If you have a large office space, pair up in two-person teams. If your office is smaller, create two sides and play capture the flag by setting up a "flag" on each end of the office. The goal is to get the opponent's flag without being struck by a marshmallow. If you're hit, you're either out permanently (we advise a rule that states you have to be hit three times to be out) or you have to remain inactive for thirty seconds before reengaging in the game. Capture that flag and bring it home to marshmallow mama!

Barely Used Client Services Position for Sale, Complete With Bent File Cabinet

Selling items on eBay is all about the description. The better job you do at explaining every detail about the item you have for sale, the better chance you have of making the sale. Buyers just want to know everything they can before they buy.

Imagine, for a moment, that you could sell, say, your job on eBay. How would you describe it? If you needed to turn your job title into sales speak, playing up the features and benefits the best you can without overplaying the "cosmetic" or "functional" damages of your position, how would you describe it? Time to find out. Sort of.

Partner up, preferably with someone who has a different but understandable job description. You are going to exchange job titles for the purposes of this exercise, and you're each going to write the job description of your partner as an eBay listing. Take pictures of the key components of the job, as you see them, and write up the job title as if you're selling the job on eBay. Remember, you're selling that specific person's job, not the position as a whole, so the job listing should come with the specifics for that person's experience with the job.

When you're done, exchange the listings and share the love. Write up how you would describe your personal job position for sale. Then, when you've had enough, throw it up on eBay and take the afternoon (and all subsequent afternoons) off.

This Is of a Melted Popsicle

Is it possible to capture opposite? For instance, can you bottle both sweet and sour tastes? Sure you can. Can you be both wet and dry? Of course. Can your wallet have both lots of money and none? Um, well, no. At least not that you've ever seen. Grab a partner and a couple of digital cameras, and see if you can capture opposites.

Each of you is to go out into your local community and capture three images of each of these opposites:

Light and **dark**
Hot and cold
Good and *evil*
Life and death
An opposite theme you get from your partner

The idea is to find three examples of each of these topics, so you'll return with fifteen pictures. When you return, share what you found and talk about why they represent both ends of the spectrum.

Lisa Dives Headfirst to Save the Highlighter From Hitting the Floor

Sports fans know of no greater video joy than a highlight reel. All the great plays of a season or a game or a race packed into a few minutes of adrenaline-filled bliss. From rim-shaking dunks to amazing catches, from walk-off home runs to shorthanded goals, highlight reels are a fan's best friend. Almost all of us are on the watching end of a highlight reel, but wouldn't it be great to be on the highlight end of the reel for once? Now's your chance.

4
PERSON EXERCISE

You are going to need just about everyone on your team to be involved in this exercise. You'll also need a digital video camcorder and access to some video-editing software, like iMovie or Movie Maker.

Your task today is to create a highlight reel of your office, environment or team, capturing them making amazing plays doing exactly what they do. If they're accountants, show them making a great accounting play. If they're designers, catch all the great designing action on tape. Set up scenarios where they can exaggerate a common action, like closing the filing cabinet with one leg or handling two client phone calls at the same time. Film all of the heart-stopping action, then head to the computer.

Use your editing software to match up the highlight montage to an awe-inspiring background track. Upload your video to YouTube and send everyone his or her own, personal highlight reel. You can sign autographs later.

Camp Sixty-Four-Page-Catalog-Production Is Open for Business

In June 2008, Disney followed up their incredibly popular *High School Musical franchise* with another musical giant, Camp Rock. *The concept is a prestigious musical summer camp that takes performing teen campers and turns them into teen rock idols. While we're sure there are summer camps all around the nation that tailor to specific genres of teen life, the concept got us thinking: What would a summer camp be like if you guys were running it? Let the games begin.*

You and two partners will be creating your own summer camp. It's a weeklong camp, filled with whatever activities and purpose you see fit...or unfit, for that matter! The only restriction is it has to have a general theme that weaves its way into everything the camp does. That theme is up to you, but the real creativity comes in the activities that all lead up to the final whatever, the last night where the big event happens. Invent the games, the activities, the schedule and the big finale. Then call Disney and see if they're interested!

Nothing breaks the post-lunch sleepies like a good, old-fashioned, interoffice treasure hunt. Get another devious soul to help you with the plan. First, you'll need some treasure. (Chocolate works like a charm.) Next, you'll need a place to hide it. (That's on you; we can't see your space.) Now you and your partner will need to develop a series of clues that will lead people to look for and find the treasure. Write a starter clue that will lead people to the next clue and the next clue, until they find the treasure. Make the clues challenging, perhaps in code or a poetic tone. (Unless the chocolate is near something hot; then, speed up the game with easier clues.) Wait until everyone has gone for lunch. Place the clues in their respective spots and leave the starter clues on the treasure hunters' desks before they return. Then sit back and watch the action!

I Found the Treasure Near the Radiator–Chocolate Ice Cream Was a Bad Choice

PowerPoint Texas Hold'em Storytelling

Like most people, you probably have a deep-rooted love for PowerPoint documents, Texas Hold'em poker and telling stories with pictures. Who doesn't? We'd be remiss if we didn't offer you and two of your closest PowerPoint/Texas Hold'em/storytelling friends an opportunity to prove it.

4 PERSON EXERCISE

First, get an unbiased party to choose five random images online and put them into a PowerPoint document, one image per slide. Send this PowerPoint document to each person in the group. These images represent your "community" images, in the same way that the five cards on the table represent the community cards that each Texas Hold'em player can use to make his or her hand. All three of you have the same five images to start, you just need to add your unique two images.

Each of you gets to choose two additional images you want to use to tell a visual story. You can place the new images wherever you'd like in the order of images, you just need to be able to tell a story that is illustrated from slide to slide. Your story can be text on each slide, it can be an audio voiceover within the PowerPoint or you can simply tell the story as you present the PowerPoint.

I'd Be an Interplanetary Starship Commander With an Eye for Appropriate Colors

In today's digital age, our job titles are a bit fuzzy. What designers do today is very different than what they did twenty years ago. A hundred years ago, a "designer" was something else all together. While nearly all of the traditional job titles given to the creative community are children of the corporate climate within the last century, the services we perform, at their core, have been around much, much longer. Let's explore that historical journey a little today.

Get two other members for your group. The three of you will be defining what your job title would be in the following eras:

Medieval times
Ancient Greece
The year 2248
Prehistoric times
Old West

The goal is to evaluate what you do, at its very core, then translate that to what was (or will be) available at the time. As an example, a designer today is a communicator, an artist and a thinker. What job titles in these eras would be your trade, and why? If you put "king" down for each one, perhaps your fantasy life slightly outweighs your real life.

First Off, My Opponent Can't Possibly Deny That Without Me, He'd Be Nuts

Peanut butter or jelly: Which is more important to the world's most famous sandwich?

The debate has raged for years, and it's time you stood up for what you believe in and take a side. Get another participant for the exercise, each taking a side on this monumental argument. Debate why you believe your ingredient is more important.

The Object of the Game Is to Hit Mike With Blank DVDs

In 1971, the first coin-operated video game was installed in the student union at Stanford University. In 1972, Atari was founded and they released the father of all console-based video games: Pong. Since then, video games have become a $10 billion industry, with millions of households gathering around the TV to play Xbox, PlayStation or Wii. Games are developed for everything from war scenarios and flight simulators to cooking challenges and dance competitions.

It's time you entered the world of video game development by grabbing a partner and collaborating to create a video game for your environment or, better yet, of your environment. Create a video game that revolves around something in your workplace or environment, considering the intended console (and what features that console provides), the point of view and scoring. Is it an action game, a role-playing game or a multiplayer, story-driven game? Who knows, you may get a call from Blizzard asking about rights!

I Call the Starbucks!
I Call the Starbucks!

4
PERSON
EXERCISE

The magical days when we were in grade school were filled with playful moments, but none were as globally anticipated and universally loved as that precious fifteen minutes we received every day at 10:37—recess! When that bell rings for recess, it's like juvenile jailbreak, baby! Kids are screaming and flailing, sprinting at top speeds to get to their favorite play area and "call it" before someone else does. It's the best fifteen minutes anyone could ever give you, and you made the most of every single moment on the playground.

There came a time, though, as we grew older, that we stopped screaming, we stopped running, we stopped flailing and sprinting and calling. Somewhere between fifth and ninth grade, we lost recess. That joy was replaced with responsibility and peer pressure and coolness. If we could somehow get recess back, wouldn't it be the greatest achievement of our lives?! Today, we can.

When we were kids, the playground called to us. Each item on the playground, from the swings to the monkey bars, was perfect for us and exactly what we wanted. But we're adults now. We need more than slides to get us excited enough to rush out of the doors of our agencies, flailing our hands and screaming at the top of our lungs. That's your task today.

Grab three other fun-loving creatives and collaborate to design the grown-up playground. What things would inspire you to rush out those doors and interact with them? What things would make up the perfect playground for you right now?

INTERVIEW WITH

Sam
HARRISON

·····•·•·••·•·••·•·•·•·•·····

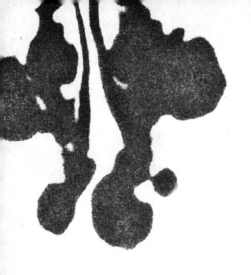

There are people in your life whom you are naturally drawn to. It's hard to put your finger on what attracts you to them, but something in their demeanor just calls to you. For virtually everyone who has had the privilege of hearing Sam Harrison speak at a conference or in a group setting, Sam's one of those people. Who would guess that behind that comfortable Georgia drawl and under that familiar baseball cap lies the harbinger of idea spotting. *Sam travels all over the country, introducing people in small corporate meeting rooms and large design conference lecture halls to the secrets of creativity on command.* His books—*Zing!: Five Steps and 101 Tips for Creativity on Command* and *IdeaSpotting: How to Find Your Next Great Idea*—have been staples in the creative community for years. With solid, applicable advice and usable, retainable techniques to generate ideas, Sam's books are every bit they claim to be and more.

Years of research and observation have given Sam the tools he needs to offer this sound advice. But how does a person begin to explore the concept of creativity and the process of creating ideas? "I'm just nosy," Sam begins. "Idea generation has fascinated me since childhood, but I don't think I began to consciously examine creativity until early in my own creative career when someone gave me a copy of James Young's *A Technique for Producing Ideas*. **There's no formula for creativity**, of course, but that book made me aware of creative process and prodded me to broadly explore creativity.

"During my years in brand communications, product development and marketing, I turned, twisted and tested all types of idea-generation techniques with myself and with my teams. Some worked wonderfully, some failed miserably. I tried to embrace the best and leave the rest. I developed a pretty good creative toolkit for myself and my teams.

"About eight years ago, I was at the point financially and mentally where I could curve away from full-time communications work. I deep-dived into the study of creativity, reading everything I could get my hands on and interviewing dozens of highly creative people. **I love helping people find the way to their own creativity.** We can't study to be creative any more than we can study to love. Carl Jung explained that the four highest human achievements—love, faith, hope and insight—can neither be taught nor learned since they come through experiences. Creativity is fueled by insights and, as Jung said, these insights are the result of experiences. **My books and talks hopefully point people toward processes and techniques providing experiences for creative insights."**

Sam is often brought in to the corporate setting to improve ideation by teaching sound idea-generation techniques. The term "brainstorming" has gotten a bad rap corporately, as team leaders have struggled to inspire their teams to be creative. Sam starts with defining the purpose of the time. "First off," Sam advises, **"it's vital for a team leader to remember the difference between a brainstorming session and a business meeting. Never the twain should meet.**

"Business meetings are primarily left-brained affairs filled with reports and spreadsheets, discussions and debates. Effective brainstorming sessions are 100 percent right-brained, packed with ideas and insights and void of judgment, egos and analysis. Brainstorming should be a place where, as creative researcher Vera John-Steiner describes, minds meet in the air.

"To help this happen, the team leader should never go into a brainstorming session with the goal of coming out with one great idea. **Brainstorming is about quantity, not quality**—the team is trying to generate lots of ideas without regard to their value or significance. To keep judgment out of the room, an editing session should be subsequent to the brainstorming session and not become part of it.

"The team leader should state the problem or goal, review the brainstorming guidelines and then

stand clear. Remember [the University of Texas quarterback] Vince Young's incredible performance in the Rose Bowl a few years ago? Afterwards, a reporter asked [head football] coach Mack Brown, 'When did Vince Young really become a star quarterback?' And the coach replied, 'When I got out of his way.' **Part of the team leader's job is to get out of the way so the team can bubble up solutions.**

"Rather than worrying too much about leading brainstorming, a team leader should focus on how to inject energy into sessions. In the film *Something's Gotta Give*, Jack Nicholson is walking on a beach with Diane Keaton and, at one point, he picks up a stone, tosses it into the air, then gives it to her. [After the director said cut and] asked why he didn't just hand her the stone to begin with, he said one of his axioms is that motion pictures should have motion.

"Likewise, I believe brainstorming should have storms and be a bit stormy—people feeling free to move around, laugh and joke, fidget with toys and toss tennis balls around the room. Anything to add energy and relax participants.

"When it comes to brainstorming, a team leader can learn a lot from the frame and flow of comedy improvisation. In an improv company, there are no stars. Everybody works on the same level, depending on each other for fuel and feedback. And improv players don't isolate themselves in silos—they riff and jam like jazz musicians, hitchhiking on fellow performers' thoughts and ideas. The same thing happens in highly productive brainstorming. In my seminars, I urge people to take a local improv workshop to expand their creativity. They'll learn lots of techniques, and they'll become much less inhibited, which is a valuable characteristic for collaboration and teamwork."

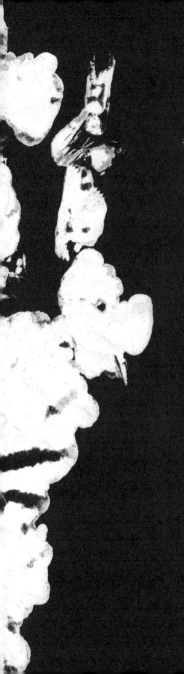

Through the years, Sam has helped thousands of team leaders extract greater creative content from their teams. **What's the secret? What's the one thing team leaders can do to facilitate the creative process?** "Try to create a climate of generosity and risk-taking," Sam says. "I've interviewed lots of highly creative people, and I've never had a single one tell me they became creative—or stayed creative—by playing it safe. **A team afraid to make mistakes is a team doomed to safety and sameness.** Of course, we're talking about good mistakes—strong effort, bad result—and not bad mistakes—sloppy effort, bad result. No team leader should tolerate lack of effort or sloppiness."

The patron saint of team creativity, Sam Harrison, has been traveling around the country, talking to folks about their creative environments. He's seen the good, the bad and the ugly, and he has some insightful advice about the power of the creative environment and how team leaders can influence the quality and quantity of their teams' ideas by paying some notice to their environments:

"We all know environments affect us—we experience mental and physical shifts each time we enter a relaxing spa, upbeat nightclub or romantic restaurant. Surroundings impact our energy and change our minds and bodies.

Go into the offices of Martha Stewart, and you dive into a sea of white—it's like a giant canvas for lively inspiration boards, shelves of colorful product samples and brainstorming tables scattered with bold fabrics. Energy gushes.

Contrast this with the offices of a certain Fortune 500 firm infamous for its militaristic environment. No employee can have more than three personal objects in his or her workspace! It's hard to believe much creative energy flows out of those cubicles. Employees probably spend most of their energy plotting a jailbreak."

Sam continues, "But there's more to developing a creative workspace than adding bells and whistles. We need to determine what workspace will best inspire and serve our particular team. I've been in some zillion-dollar, flashy studios that feel sterile and hollow and some bare-bones places packed with energy. There are no automatic correlations. It's all about what works best for the team that uses the workspace. Bottom line: Does the space match the vision and values of the people who work there?

When looking at space, it's also helpful to ponder it from the perspective of what [psychologist] James Gibson refers to as 'affordance'—what the space and objects afford the team, such as reading, working, designing, playing, relaxing and so forth. That way, we're viewing the workplace as active energy rather than static space.

The space must also inspire and facilitate interaction and collaboration. This is a priority at Googleplex, where even the stairways become places for people to meet and work—they actually have laptop portals built into the steps!

But you don't have to go high-tech or spend millions of dollars to make interactions happen—at Sundance Institute, outdoor picnic tables become meeting places for directors, writers and actors. Robert Redford has the money to make Sundance polished and plush, but he feels the rustic furnishings inspire people to be more resourceful.

Art also matters, of course, and not just what we hang on the walls. Art includes the colors, forms, music and other elements affecting all our senses. In some cases, we can recharge our creative energy just by changing the music or rearranging existing art and furniture so we notice it again.

One of the best examples of how space can boost creative energy is one I heard Malcolm Gladwell tell about Kent Beck, a legendary computer programmer. Kent was asked by a printing company to help them work through some technology problems they couldn't solve.

Kent got there and found everybody working separately, so he told them to find a space where they could all work together. The team found a corner of a machine room and began working there several hours every day. They soon solved the technology problems.

Kent later told Malcolm: 'They hired me for my technical expertise, but telling them to rearrange the furniture was the most valuable thing I could offer.'"

4
PERSON
EXERCISE

The Par 3 Ninth Hole Keeps Going to the Copier

That support pole by Scott's desk is calling to you. You hear it every day, whispering "I bet you can't hit me with a paper plate from the end of the hall!" Your coworkers have heard it, too, but from other places in the office. The corner of the cutting desk, the tree by accounting, that really skinny intern in production. You hear them mocking you, as if you don't have the power to turn the switch and convert your average, ordinary office environment into the greatest paper-plate Frisbee golf course the world has ever seen! **So what are you waiting for?**

Set up a nine-hole course that includes tee boxes and flags. Make the flags and tape them to the objects you need to hit in order to score. Take ordinary paper plates, stand at the first tee box and let 'er fly! Like regular golf, the lowest score wins. The object is to hit the target in as few attempts as possible, standing on the plate's resting spot after each throw. **Fore!**

I've Got Two in the Front Row by the Projector, Who Wants 'Em?

There's nothing less impressive than receiving an e-mail invitation to a meeting. Most calendar programs send them automatically. They're cold and lack a certain human element. They also fail miserably at getting people pumped about the meeting. You could schedule a "How we're going to split up the $3 million jackpot we just won" meeting, and if an e-mail is sent out as a reminder, you'll still get the grumpy meeting walk. What you need is a boost, something to get people excited about the event. And what says excitement like replacing those boring meeting e-mails with...a ticket!

Everyone loves tickets. Tickets mean that it's a real event, something people want to go to. It's so popular, in fact, that tickets had to be made to only let in the truly elite... those who have a ticket. Tickets mean you are on the inside, you have a guaranteed seat in the event of the century! It's time to make up some tickets.

Grab a ticket-thirsty partner to help you with the exercise. You'll fist need to identify a stinker event coming up on the docket. Then, you'll need to decide how you're going to make your tickets. You can do it digitally or you can draw them up by hand. Some proprietary element, like a photo or a piece of artwork, will ensure people will want to keep their tickets, and it will help against counterfeiters. Cut just enough tickets for the event, and pass them out only to those who are worthy to attend the event. On the day of the event, plant a guy outside the conference room door to ward off scalpers. Enjoy the event!

The Treasure Lies Hidden
Beneath a Spout of Bavarian Hops

Lisa Duty of Ravenchase Adventures in Richmond, Virginia, creates live-action hunts using homemade treasure maps, clues written in code, actors placed along the journey and gadgets like **black** lights to lead teams throughout the city in search of a treasured prize. It's time you got in on the fun and put together your own adventure.

This exercise encourages two parts to the game: a story and a live-action component. Let's start with the story. Grab a fellow storyteller and create a story that can be executed in two parts. The first part will be acted out on video, the second part will be a hunt in your community to find the answers or treasure.

The story you need to develop should have an element of something missing, like a treasure that needs to be found. The story could be one that describes how the treasure was lost, or perhaps the story of someone searching for the treasure in the present time. Whatever direction you decide you go, there needs to be an element that stops the story and allows your participants to continue the story on foot.

The second part to the exercise is the live play. You'll need to hide the treasure in the community, and then create clues that lead to access points, which reveal additional clues. Five or six clues and destinations are usually enough to create a two- or three-hour game. Make sure you leave an "out" if the participants get stuck on a clue or make a wrong turn by providing a phone number they can call to get back on track.

217

Surprise! There Really Is a Killer Behind the Door!

We've all seen movies where the development of the plot leads to something unbelievable, something that would never happen if you were in that situation. Open to a dark, wooded forest, creepy noises everywhere. Suddenly, the main character hears a scream coming from an old, abandoned shack. He slowly walks closer to the front door, and he hears another blood-curdling cry from behind the door. Inexplicably, the main character decides to **OPEN THE DOOR AND GO INSIDE!** Why would he do that?! Blood-curdling shrieks = world-record sprint in the opposite direction. Everyone on the planet knows this...except the main character. We all know how we would react in certain movie situations, and now we're going to prove it.

You're going to need as many other people for your team as actors and actresses in the movie you're going to mock. You will need to choose a movie scene that progresses in a very different way than you would have progressed. For instance, you may choose the famous courtroom scene from *A Few Good Men*, where Tom Cruise and Jack Nicholson are jawing back and forth and Jack Nicholson's character finally snaps and yells, "You can't handle the truth!" Perhaps you would have responded differently when Tom Cruise's character was interrogating you. You may choose to be funny or react inappropriately. Whatever scene you choose, you're going to get a chance to fix it.

First, choose a scene, and then decide how you would have changed that scene with your own brand of reaction. Use your team to set up and film the new scene on a digital video camera. If you have a way to record the original movie onto a computer, record your scene. If you don't have the ability to record the scene, play the scene on a high-quality TV and record it off the TV with your digital video camera. Cut the movie at that fateful point and insert your new edit.

2

PERSON EXERCISE

Let's Go Down to the "Slaughter Your Own Meal" Buffet Tonight

Themed restaurants are all the rage. You can dine with Disney characters, snack in a café built in the deep rain forest, complete with animatronic gorillas and elephants, blast off to deep space and enjoy atomic meatballs, or watch knights joust while you tear into your turkey leg. The food at themed restaurants is often traditional fare tagged with themed names, but occasionally, the grub is part of the experience. Most of the time, that experience is a favorable one, or, at the very least, it didn't suck. But what if it did?

Get another willing participant to help you with this exercise. The two of you will collaborate to develop a very bad idea for a themed restaurant. Imagine a theme that is as unappetizing as you can think of, and design a restaurant around it. Come up with the name, the environment and the menu. Make it as doomed an idea as there ever could be. Who knows? There's something for everyone, right?

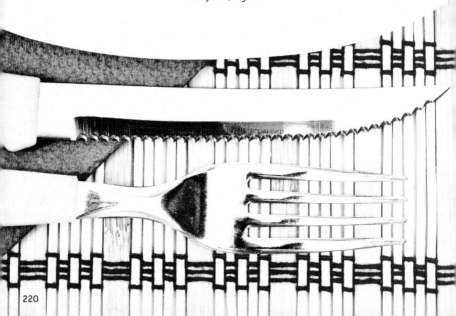

Are You Going to Be a Cheapskate on This Project, Too?

Every new client project gets a client project questionnaire. It's the process for thousands of creative agencies across the nation. The questionnaire gives insight and a baseline to the project and tells us what we're making and for whom we're making it. It has questions like "Who is the intended audience?" and "What are the three most important things to communicate?" These questionnaires provide valuable information, but they could be so much more fun, couldn't they? If you said "yes" with a slightly devious smile, then continue.

Get a partner to help with the exercise. You two are going to develop the world's worst client project questionnaire. The questions you ask are to be hideously inappropriate, questions that would never be uttered to a client...ever! The questionnaire will be half truth and half shock, but all fun. Develop the kind of questions that cut through the ordinary and get right down to the core of the project. Just make sure you don't accidentally send this one instead of the real one.

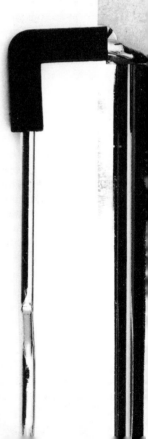

This Patch Makes the Office Coffee Taste Like Starbucks

In 1979, the FDA approved the first commercially available prescription patch, issued to fight motion sickness by releasing specific doses of medication into the bloodstream through the skin. Since then, patches have been used for everything from nicotine dependency to antidepressants. While the skin provides a pretty effective barrier, the patch has become a viable method for medication delivery.

Wouldn't it be nice if we could use a patch to alleviate the symptoms of many of the things that cause us grief in the workplace? Imagine a patch that could drown out the annoying voice from the cubicle next to you, or one that would administer the correct dosage of Red Bull to you throughout the day. The patch could have many uses in your environment or industry, if you were brave enough to create them. Which, of course, you are!

Grab a willing participant for your mad scientist creative laboratory experiment today. The two of you will be collaborating to develop a series of five fictional patches that you could sell within your environment that would alleviate various problems your unique environment presents. It doesn't matter how it works, it only matters that it works, so be inventive. Hopefully you don't develop a patch that makes creative exercises go away.

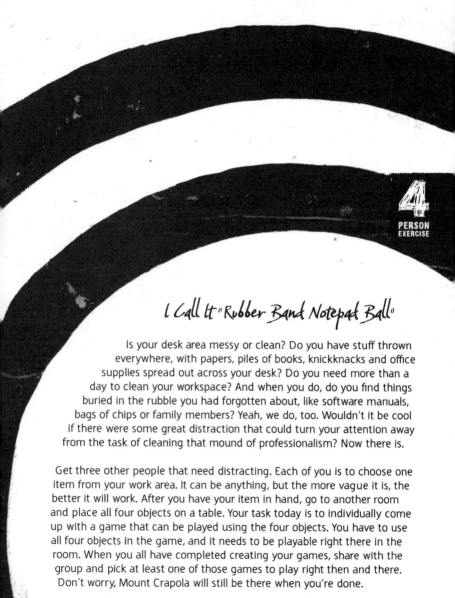

I Call It "Rubber Band Notepad Ball"

Is your desk area messy or clean? Do you have stuff thrown everywhere, with papers, piles of books, knickknacks and office supplies spread out across your desk? Do you need more than a day to clean your workspace? And when you do, do you find things buried in the rubble you had forgotten about, like software manuals, bags of chips or family members? Yeah, we do, too. Wouldn't it be cool if there were some great distraction that could turn your attention away from the task of cleaning that mound of professionalism? Now there is.

Get three other people that need distracting. Each of you is to choose one item from your work area. It can be anything, but the more vague it is, the better it will work. After you have your item in hand, go to another room and place all four objects on a table. Your task today is to individually come up with a game that can be played using the four objects. You have to use all four objects in the game, and it needs to be playable right there in the room. When you all have completed creating your games, share with the group and pick at least one of those games to play right then and there. Don't worry, Mount Crapola will still be there when you're done.

INTERVIEW WITH

Jenn and Ken Visocky O'Grady

||||||| OF |||||||

ENSPACE

||||||||||||||||||||

← Ken   Jenn →

Small agencies live and die by their processes. While there may be some room in a larger agency for the creative process to be made up of competing forces, the small agency has to be lean, focused and 100 percent bought in to the way they approach ideas. Even the smallest hiccup or selfish motivation is magnified by the ripples it projects. In short, small agencies have to sell out to the vision.

If there's only one thing you remember about Enspace, it's that they're sold out to the idea of group buy-in to the creative process. **They work as a team, they ideate as a team, they succeed as a team and they fail as a team.** And when they say "team," they mean clients, vendors, freelancers and even family.

Jenn and Ken Visocky O'Grady started Enspace in 1998, and their work has done nothing but win award after award since. The husband-and-wife team runs this small yet powerful shop from their stylish loft space in Cleveland's Creative Corridor. Five minutes with the pair and it's easy to see how this small shop produces such big ideas.

Jenn and Ken are huge advocates of collaborative design, the philosophy of "working with" rather than "working for" or "working on." **The agency model is one of family.** In reality, they are family, both literally and figuratively. This collaborative, family approach has fostered inner-agency and client relationships well beyond the bond most agencies share. "Over the years," Jenn begins, "we've developed a few little tricks that we can get away with that larger firms can't, just by the nature of our personal relationships. Everyone at Enspace is fully invested in

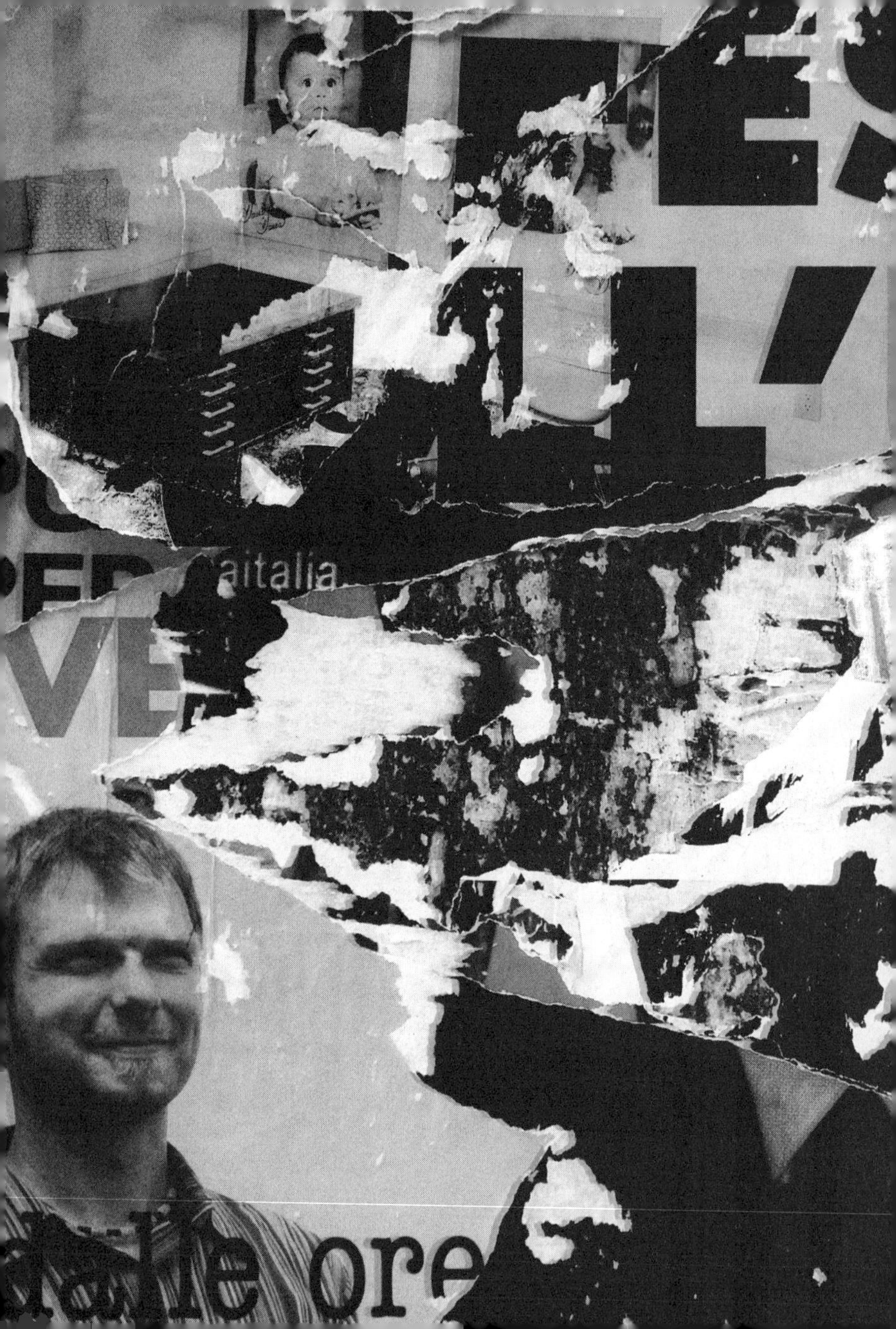
ES
aitalia
VE
dalle ore

each other's success. It's like working with family. We call each other out when we see bullpuckey. We ground each other from our comfortable little graphic tricks, things like font choice or use of color, paper, whatever. This helps keep the work moving forward, and it keeps people from getting stuck in ruts.

"We also pass work around the office. If one of us gets stuck on a project, we'll put it up on the file server and ask someone else to take a crack at it. We think this helps keep the work fresh, increases our production time and takes a lot of the ego out of the office. Enspace belongs to us collectively. The work belongs to Enspace. It's about the studio and not the individuals."

Their size and collaborative philosophy allow them to define and hone their creative process without endangering the flow of the team. They can set aside a specific time to formally generate ideas while still allowing the space everyone needs to ideate on their own. "We set aside a scheduled time to meet," Jenn explains, "so everyone knows it's coming. That gives us time to prepare, and notice to bring those right-before-I-fell-asleep ideas to the table. We start with caffeine, comfy chairs, lots of sketch paper and good snacks, and we usually start early. Then there's the lure of adventure lunch, out of the office, midday. So the whole brainstorming day is built around reward. We get to hang out, we get to be goofy, we get fed.

"We then spend some controlled time [sometimes with an egg timer for the ticking] 'sketching,' which means something different for everyone. Some of us draw, some of us list, some work out ideas in loose paragraphs, etc. We work in pretty short bursts, put work up on the critique wall, compare, then revisit. Often, we'll circle a few things that are working best on each sheet, and then have another team member run with those ideas for another burst of sketch time. We've found that those oh-I-wish-I'd-thought-of-that ideas can really get the whole team excited, and that if you guard them like they're personal property, then they don't get fully developed.

"When we're in active brainstorming mode, it's all about generating ideas. That means that nothing gets shot down. Some things get moved forward, but we all really work to avoid negativity, or closing down an idea before it gets legs. We'll spend enough of the project's development filing the idea to a point, so there's an understanding that the first brainstorming session isn't really the place for that. We think of it as filling the bucket."

Another advantage to the small-team environment is the ability to get to know your team at deeper levels than large agencies can do. Through this experience, Jenn and Ken have found that looking at the team like a coach would, learning what motivates each individual separately to achieve the best results corporately, is a vital characteristic of effective creative leadership. "We saw a great speaker at a HOW conference a couple of years back," Ken reveals, "talking about a predictive personality index. The core concept was that we all have basic and specific needs that drive us, and that while we all grow and develop, our core needs remain the same. If you can spend some time getting to know your team, you'll find that some of them like structure, others need flexibility, some really like public praise, others work for bonuses...you get the idea. Combine your own core values— how you'd like to be treated—with an individual's needs, and you'll know how to communicate with people.

"We'd all pick inspiration over discipline every time. Hierarchal structure kills creativity. Build a team of leaders. Seek opportunities for each and every member of that team to grow dramatically. Don't guard your position. Instead, imagine the power of your team when each individual is doing what they do best. Share everything you know, and make a habit of actively learning more."

By the sound of it, they've already learned a lifetime's worth.

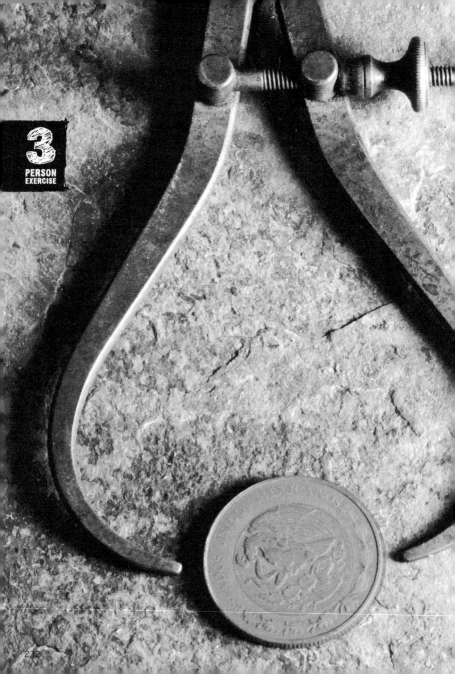

My Quarter Starts With a Potpie Crust

There are a lot of coins out there, and they all have qualities and characteristics that are similar. We can identify a coin by touch by these characteristics. Isn't it time we redesigned the coin? (Say "yes." Good answer!)

You and two partners are going to redesign a coin one feature at a time. Start off by drawing the shape, then pass the paper to the next person, who is charged with adding one feature. Pass it to the third person to add another feature. Go around a few times until it gets difficult to think of anything to add, then go around one last time adding features that may be a bit off the wall. Who knows...maybe kids in the twenty-ninth century will be collecting your creation!

The Madison Avenue Medicine Show

In the early to mid-nineteenth century, traveling medicine men would peddle magical elixirs that promised to cure ails and reinvigorate life. Shouted from the deck of wagon-wheeled carts, these showmen would promise health and prosperity through bottles of oils and tonics, weaving tales of incredible recovery and gargantuan vitality. Rarely more than sugar water or fish oil, the power of suggestion was often enough to simulate effectiveness. But the pitch was profitable, for sure!

Get another willing showman (or showwoman) for this exercise. Your task is to create the magical elixir that cures the symptoms of your choice of corporate ailments. Collaborate with your partner to create the office ailment of choice for your situation. Then create the "pitch" for this bottled tonic, writing the tale of the ailment, the cure and the stories of success, to convince others to purchase the elixir. You can do this together or individually, where one person writes the pitch the other designs the bottle and label or wagon/stage environment. After you have completed the task, slap on that top hat and let the peddling begin!

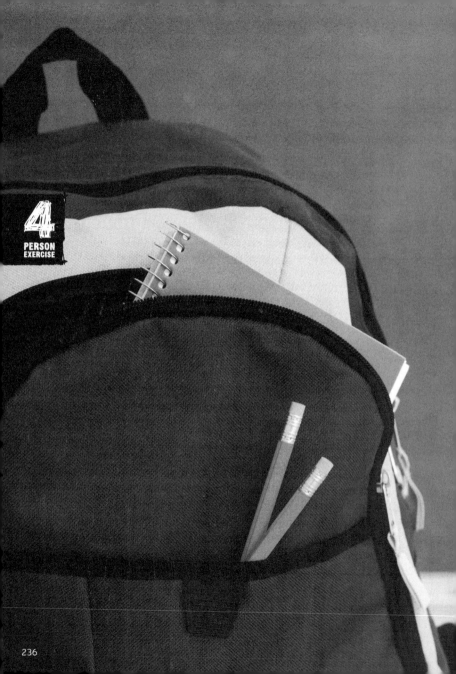

The Better Mousetrap

In 1999, *ABC News Nightline* did a feature on IDEO, one of the most innovative industrial-product design firms in the world. The purpose of the piece was to demonstrate the process of designing a better product by giving IDEO an assignment and filming their creative process. The assignment was to design a better shopping cart. What IDEO came up with was remarkable, but it was their creative process that became the hero of the story.

They gathered together to discuss the problem at hand by collaborating to define a small number of definable character issues with the shopping cart, like mobility, durability, purpose and convenience. They then divided their team into small groups to go out into the community and investigate these issues, each team taking an issue. They returned to share their findings and begin the process of ideation.

After throwing around ideas on possible obstacles and solutions for each issue, they divided back into their original groups and began creating prototypes for each issue. Sketches, clay models, papier-mâché, anything to get the point across to the team what they suggested as solutions to the issue they were assigned. After coming back together and deciding what solutions worked together and what should be sidelined, the team collaborated once again to design and build the actual shopping cart.

This same creative process can be applied to any design problem simply by dividing tasks, collaborating with intent and releasing ownership of ideas to the group. That will be the core of this exercise.

Your task today is to redesign the common school backpack.

Collaborate to identify the core character issues school kids deal with in regard to the backpack. Split up either individually or in groups (depending on the size of your group) and take an issue and investigate it as thoroughly as time allows. Get back together and discuss your findings and possible solutions for each. Divide up again and develop, either on paper or in some tangible form, the solution or solutions for that issue. Reconnect and put those together to design the better backpack.

Depending on how much time you have, this could span a few minutes, a few hours or a few days. Choose the time frame you feel gets the most of out the exercise.

And Then David Pulled Up His Shorts and Went Home

Nothing breaks the ice in a conversation between two people who just met like sharing embarrassing moments. Every one of us has had moments that are too funny not to be shared. Oh, they weren't funny at the time, but looking back on them now, the embarrassment has turned to a strange sense of pride for being able to look back at yourself and laugh. In the end, very few things are funnier than embarrassing things that have happened...to other people.

You'll need a fellow storyteller for this exercise. The two of you are going to write about the most embarrassing moment...of the other person. Don't worry if you know this person that well, or even if you don't, because this moment is completely fabricated. Make up a story of the most embarrassing moment your fellow participant has ever had. Try to weave what you know of the person's real life into the story, but fabricate the embarrassing moment entirely. Hopefully, you're not right.

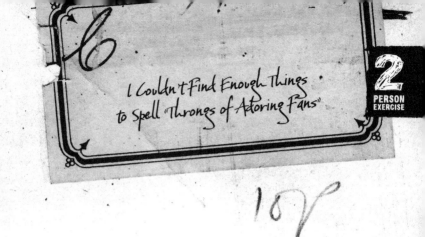

I Couldn't Find Enough Things to Spell "Throngs of Adoring Fans"

Cryptography is the practice and study of hiding information. We've all played games and solved puzzles that start with one thing that is meant to lead you to the answer. Movies have been made revolving around cryptography, like *Goonies*, *National Treasure* and *The Da Vinci Code*. The idea is to hide the answer to something solvable in plain sight. We're going to have a little fun with a form of cryptography today.

Get a partner and a digital camera for each of you. First, you're going to need to come up with the puzzle to be solved. You each need to answer this question for yourself in a single word:

What do I want right now?

Don't tell your partner what your answer is. Each of you is to go out into your environment or community and take a picture of something that starts with or stands for each letter in your word. When you finish, return to your office and print each photo, laying them on a table or pinning them up to a wall in the order that spells your word. Try and guess what the answer is to each other's puzzle.

›interview with‹

Debbie Millman

STERLING BRANDS

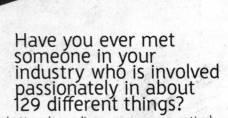

Have you ever met someone in your industry who is involved passionately in about 129 different things?

To make matters worse, (or better, depending on your perspective) they are really good at every one of the things they do. Every industry makes their own heroes, but these talented few are deserving of the role, as they lift up the industry in so many ways. In the pantheon of design, there are but a numbered few that could point to their body of work and it alone would merit the place at the table.

Meet Debbie Millman.

Although you've probably already met her—when you're involved in as much as Debbie is, it's hard not to have crossed paths. Her day job is as Partner and President of Sterling Brands in New York. As if that didn't take up enough of her time and energy, she's also the host of her own radio show, "Design Matters;" she teaches at the School of Visual Arts; she is the coauthor of the über-popular Speak Up blog; she's on the national AIGA board; and she's authored two books on design ... in the last two years.

So ... what did you do today?

It's impossible to separate the creative from the passion in Debbie's case: It's why she has enough energy to walk down so many streets. And while she is passionate toward so many things in the design community, she is a passionate leader to her team at Sterling Brands. Her experience leading groups of people—whether it is within an intimate classroom setting or the tens of thousands of creatives that read Speak Up or listen to "Design Matters"—has proved fruitful for Sterling Brands and the team she leads. How does she manage to mold the individual creative processes of some of the most talented creatives in the nation into one cohesive Sterling Brands process? "The short answer is 'I really don't have to do much of anything,'" Debbie begins. **"The individual processes are now fundamentally necessary in order to do really innovative work.**

"Design isn't just about design anymore. There is no more 'mass market' in which to target a product. There is no one demographic picture of the planet. I recently saw cultural anthropologist Grant McCracken speak, and he discussed how lifestyle typologies expanded to first 3, then 6, then 9 and then 12 typologies—there is now too much variation and we have reached categorical exhaustion. As a result, I have come to believe that the term 'design' ultimately undermines the job we do as consultants, marketers, creators and strategists. **Design is not only about design; it is now the perfect, meticulously crafted balance of cultural anthropology, behavioral psychology, commerce and creativity.**

It is about cultural anthropology because what we do in our culture—whether it is an obsession with reality television or weapons of mass destruction—has a major impact on the brands around us. It is about psychology because if we don't fundamentally understand the brain circuitry of our audience and really know what they are thinking—and why they are thinking it!—we will not be able to solicit their imagination. It is about commerce, because understanding the marketplace and the messaging impacts and influences perception. It is about creativity, because if we don't create a compelling package, then consumers won't notice it and buy it.

"With all this in mind, I encourage robust discourse and dialogue in my teams and deliberately put people in teams that can further the ideas and the deliverable beyond what is expected," Debbie says.

Like all successful creative leaders, Debbie and Sterling Brands have a purposeful philosophy and plan for idea generation. As she puts it, "Idea generation is best encouraged with fun, safe, warm and encouraging environments.

Dull focus-group-room-type-facilities actually kill ideas, rather than encourage them, so we want a lot of light, a lot of laughter and a lot of sharing to come up with new ideas."

When it comes to the actual brainstorming session, Debbie has five pieces of advice for anyone leading an idea meeting:

1. Focus on ideas versus deliverables. Brainstorming should be about perceptions, not preferences.

2. When brainstorming, make allowances for familiarity. People are generally more comfortable with what they know. And human beings, as a species, tend to be frightened of change.

3. Brainstorming is an art, not a science. Try and investigate emotional connections and design sensibilities. Avoid an overdependence on thinking "It can't be done" or the "Prove it can work" mentality.

4. More is definitely merrier. Brainstorming is a time to develop scenarios, not solve problems. Come up with as many ideas as possible.

5. Never say NO. A brainstorm is the time for ideas, not solutions.

That last piece of advice is tough for many creatives and leaders alike to swallow. We're so wired to find answers in a complete form that we often by-pass nuggets of very good ideas that simply need to be grown into something greater. It's an extremely relevant piece of advice for young creative team leaders. What other advice would Debbie give to these young guns?

"DO NOT COMPROMISE,"

Debbie forcefully warns. "I'd ask them to consider what they would do if they knew they would never fail and to pursue that as if their lives depended on it, because it does! Your twenties and thirties are not times to be compromising, either with work or with ideas! **Do what you love and challenge yourself to do something that can change the world."**

Fuh-Get-Uh-Bowdit

DDB Chicago is the ad agency that brought us Bud Light's Dude" TV campaign. The campaign features a Bud Light-lovin' guy who communicates in completely different ways by only using the word "dude," the universal language of guys. There are 297 meanings to the word "dude," depending on the context. (We know. We counted.) If you walk into a curiously stinky room that your friend is occupying, you might say "dude," which means "Man, you reek! Why did you do that?!" You may walk into a large sports stadium for the first time and, with big eyes and a reverent tone, utter "dude," which means "Wow, I'm in awe of this place. And they have foot-long hot dogs!" It's all in the inflection, a concept we're going to explore a little today.

Get a partner and a video camera. You are going to tell a story with only one word. What word is up to you. Come up with a word or phrase that has many different meanings, depending on how it's used and the inflection in the voice. Once you've established your word or phrase, develop a story where one of you is the main character and the other is the cameraman. Create your story by shooting the different scenes and scenarios that the main character engages in when the one word is used, but make sure it's telling a story and not just showing random scenarios. You should be able to put the scenes back to back and follow a story line, with just one word of dialogue. Dude!

And How Did You Dislodge Caitlyn From the Copier Machine?

Author and creative coach Sam Harrison wrote in his book *Zing!: Five Steps and 101 Tips for Creativity on Command* that "Collaboration is a lot like improvisation, and with an improv company, there is no star. If the team doesn't win in improv, neither does the individual. Likewise with a creative team." Sam has said that he often will suggest creatives take improv classes to hone their ability to create ideas on the fly and collaborate effectively. Let's combine a little improv with another tried-and-true discovery method: the interview.

You'll need one other player in this exercise. You are going to perform a mock interview of your partner, as if you're a reporter trying to get answers to some event or occurrence. What event or occurrence, you ask? That's part of the improv. Start off by holding a fake microphone in your hand and talking into it, setting up the interview with your partner. Don't pre-conceive what you are going to ask, simply ask the questions that come to mind as you are engaged in the conversation. Be swift to take your partner's responses and add your next question. The interviewee should respond in an improv manner as well, reacting to the questions being asked and delivering the responses. Feed off one another until the interview comes to a close. Back to you in the studio, Wendy!

First, You Climb Brian's Office Wall, Then You Take the Rope Swing to Glen's Cube

Fast-food restaurants across the country feature one thing all kids want with their micro-cooked meals. No, not fries in the shapes of woodland creatures. We're talking about the play gym. These monstrosities of colorful plastic tubing are a paradise of fun for six-year-olds, with tunnels to climb through, slides to tumble down and mesh walls to conquer. But why should kids have all the fun? Ask any play-loving adult who has ever had to retrieve a scared child in the belly of the play-gym monster, and they'll tell you it's kind of fun...if it were bigger, of course. Too many double cheeseburgers and we're likely to get lodged in the Tunnel-O-Slim.

Your task today is to rework that staple of fast-food activity for you and your mates there at work. Grab another participant for this exercise. The two of you need to plan out how you would build a giant play gym within the space of your environment. The only restriction is that you can't disturb the working folks by moving them; you have to build the play gym around the office dwellers, yourself included. You can take a photo of your space and draw over it, or you can sketch it out on a piece of paper. Mix in any combination of tubes and slides, ropes and climbs, even the occasional bridge if you should need it. Just don't put the end of the slide on your boss's desk.

I'll Start With Client Sarcasm, and Then I'll Have the Presentation, Medium Rare

4 PERSON EXERCISE

Restaurant menus are usually divided up by types of food, like appetizers, salads, entrées, etc. This compartmentalizes the selections and allows guests to easily find the types of food they're looking for. Wouldn't it be interesting if what you did for a living was organized the same way? In the services sector, especially in the creative community, the services we offer are typically not line-item types of things, as they involve a great deal of strategy, design decisions, trial and error and critiques.

But if we had to create a menu for this business of ours, what would it look like? How would we split up the things we do into typical restaurant food divisions? What would an appetizer be? What would dessert be? That's your task today.

Get three other participants and split up the menu into these categories:

Appetizers
Soups and salads
Entrées
Desserts

Each of your gets one section, and you are to take what you do for a living and split it up into orderable items. Remember the scale and purpose of each of the courses listed above. The entrées are the meals, they're the big stuff, while the appetizers are meant to whet your appetite. The listings should be in that same relationship.

Where would "do creative exercises" be, and does it come with a side?

It's a Grape-Juice Shopping Cart Pushed by a One-Legged Meerkat

Ever been at a meal somewhere and noticed the food stains on the tablecloth or the coffee stains on the table? Sometimes, these stains can be quite beautiful in their randomness. Like looking at the shapes of clouds, we often personify the shapes into recognizable forms. But even with the finite shape of something like a cloud, different people see different things in their shapes, proof that experience and perspective give each of us a unique view on the world.

Let's explore this concept a little today. First, you'll need another willing participant. The two of you will be creating a stain, then exchanging the stains to apply your own perspective to it and turn it into something else.

Get a piece of paper and find something that you can use to stain the paper. Keep it to something with a relatively thin consistency. The heavier and more oil that is in the stain agent, the harder it will be to draw over it. Coffee or juice would work well. Each of you is to create your own stain on separate pieces of paper. Once the stain has dried, exchange papers and spend some time looking at the stain. Turn it around, look at it from all angles, then grab a pencil and make that stain into something. When you're done, share your creations... perhaps over a cup of coffee or juice!

2 PERSON EXERCISE

This Is Designywood—Everybahdy's Got a Dream

Tread the streets of Hollywood at just about any time of year and you'll be presented with multiple opportunities to purchase a tourist map that leads to the major tourist highlights of the area, as well as some promised "secret" locations, like movie stars' homes and points of historical interest along the way, true or not. Following the map generally provides some insight into the area, even if that insight isn't always reliable information. If nothing else, it makes for some entertaining stories.

There are probably some entertaining stories that could be told of your environment as well. If there isn't, the questionable nature of the information provides an acceptable forum for great entertainment. Your task today is to create a tourist map of your office or studio. First, grab a partner to help with the exercise. Next, draw up a crude map of your area. After you have the map, start filling in the "points of interest." Start with the highlights that anyone coming to your office shouldn't miss. Then start supplementing this with second-tier attractions. Lastly, add a few historical references along the way, likely with a less-than-average chance of them being true. When you're done, set up a booth at the door and make your fortune!

3
PERSON
EXERCISE

Ever sat at a bus stop in the rain and thought, "Didn't they see this coming?" Or decide to take rapid transit to the beach only to sit and wait at a bus-stop bench that is hotter than Hansel? (Crude *Zoolander* reference, sorry.) The fact is, bus stops get overlooked as opportunities for creative solutions. Depending on what area of the country you are in, what the climate is like and what the culture will embrace, there are some fantastic things that can be done with bus stops. You're about to talk about some of them right now!

Get a couple partners to do the exercise with you. The three of you are going to come up with the ideal bus stop for various regions of the country. First, pick a place from the list below where your new bus stop will reside:

Southern California
New York City
Miami
Kansas City
Seattle
Chicago
Las Vegas

Now collaborate to either design or list features for the new bus stop. The only restriction is that it has to retain its primary purpose, which is to provide a place to wait for the bus. There are no budget restrictions, so have at it, mass-transiters!

4
PERSON
EXERCISE

Extra! Extra! Read All About Joe Breaking the Inkjet!

If you're a regular reader of *The Onion* (www.theonion.com) and its heavily satirical approach to news, you know how much fun it can be to read absurd stories written in newsworthy ways.

Imagine if your agency or environment had a newspaper, and it reported on all the absurd happenings you're sure to have. Sounds like fun, huh? Time to step up to the plate.

You and three partners will be creating a newspaper for your environment, and it's up to you how far to take it. The bare minimum is for the four of you to name your newspaper and divide up at least four sections that each person will head up, such as front page, sports, business, classifieds, local and entertainment. Each person should, at the very least, write the lead story for his or her section. If you're feeling saucy, you can create an entire first page to each section and start taking subscriptions!

Robbie's Area Is the Sit-Up Barn for the Next Thirty Minutes

3
PERSON
EXERCISE

There's just too much work to do to carve out significant time to exercise. You've been using that excuse for the last two years, and so far, it's working. Except that bulbous midriff is pushing you farther and farther away from your keyboard, so maybe you should rethink that reasoning. If you could just take off the time it takes to go to the gym, change into your workout gear, run the gamut of your workout, shower, change back into work attire, then drive all the way back to the office, it would be easier. It sure would be ideal if there was a workout facility right there in your office, huh? Guess what? There is. You just haven't created it yet.

You're going to need a partner or two to assist in the exercise. The task is to create an office workout map. You're going to be turning your environment into a gym, where you can perform a series of exercises by using what your environment already features. You can't modify anything, meaning you can't turn desks over or move furniture, but you can use objects in the exercises. You and your team have to evaluate the space and see how it can be used for sit-ups, pull-ups, push-ups, leg extensions, squats, flys...whatever exercises you can dream up in your space. Try to create as complete a workout as you can, maybe dividing muscle groups by days.

Now, here's the true test of what you've created: Actually do it!

The Printer Will Only Print in Red Tomorrow

Do you think if fortune cookies didn't have fortunes in them, and therefore were just called "Asian cookies" or something, that they'd be as popular as they are? Don't think too hard, you'll hurt yourself. The answer is no, it's the fortune that makes them so popular. The problem with fortune cookies is that the fortunes are typically so vague, you're assured that they will come true. Cracking open a fortune cookie that reveals you will travel a short distance soon is a pretty good bet, since you have to travel said short distance to get home from the Chinese place where you're eating that cookie. Let's change the vague nature of the fortune cookies and create ones that actually mean something.

Get a partner for this exercise and collaborate to create a series of fortune cookie fortunes round one of these themes:

Your agency or work environment
Client relations Your occupation or field
Odd human behavior
Restroom etiquette

After you've created ten to fifteen fortunes, take the next step and hop on the Internet to find one of a gazillion fortune cookie recipes and make the cookies. Make them to give away at your place of business or as Christmas presents, unless you predicted you'd lose a client—then keep that to yourself.

Where's That Squashed Bug?

In your everyday environment, places where you all congregate or are familiar with, each person is to take three pictures of a detail. Look around to find some pattern or shape or object in your environment that you may have overlooked at first glance. It could be a close-up of the pattern on the floor of the entrance, the shadow a frame makes on the wall, the stain of a wine glass dropped at the Christmas party in 2004, anything that you may not have seen before. After taking these images, send them around or post them to a common area for all four of you to see. Each person must try to determine what the pictures are of. Who knows, by re-seeing what you bypass every day, you may find the inspiration for that next project you're looking for.

And "Two Bucks for a Stuck-Up Duck" Wins by a Beak!

4 PERSON EXERCISE

There is a powerful combination of speed and agility that has people all over the world spending inordinate amounts of money to take part. Of course, we're talking about racing rubber ducks, but you knew that. Racing and rubber ducks go together like peanut butter and hot dogs. They simply belong together. And today, you're going to get the opportunity to compete at the highest level you've most likely ever competed at: **the Super-Exclusive Regional Rubber Duck-Off.** Ladies and gentlemen...start your quackers!

Everyone in the group is each going to design (read: decorate) his or her very own rubber duck, then race said ducks to determine the Supreme Duck. You'll need a rubber duck for each contestant, a body of water to race in, and some ground rules. You need to decide ahead of time if current or design will power your ducks. If the only body of water you have available is a still body of water, you'll need to design in how the ducks will move, either by wind or by motor. If you have a body of water with a current, it is advised to make this a duck-only affair, no propulsion needed.

Once each of you has designed the perfect racing duck, get the race started and see who comes out Supreme Duck!

I Used a Skeleton Key, You Used a Door

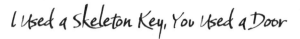

Just because we're out in public doesn't mean certain natural, human urgencies are gone. I'm talking about needing to use the restroom. Most public restrooms are separated by sex, save for the occasional unisex restroom. Differentiating which restroom we should choose is pretty simple: look for the icon on the door. The men's restroom looks oddly enough like a man, while the women's restroom...you guessed it, looks like a woman. We learn which icon to choose pretty early.

But if we lived, say, in medieval times, would we know the icons we use today are meant to separate the restrooms? Suspend the fact that there weren't separate restrooms in medieval times, what icons would we use to communicate which outhouse is the men's and which is the women's? That will be your task today.

Grab another participant for this exercise and choose a theme, or a series of themes, from the list below to start with:

Medieval times
Wild, wild West
Ancient Rome
Prehistoric times
Under the sea
Futuristic space
Major sports
On safari

After choosing a theme or themes, divide up who will do the men's and who will do the women's. Create the iconic restroom sign for that theme. And wash your hands after.

interview with

Lisa Duty

Ravenhurst
Adventure

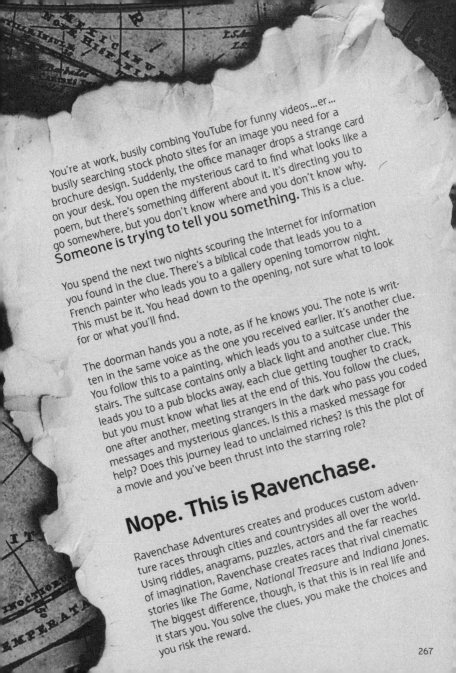

You're at work, busily combing YouTube for funny videos...er... busily searching stock photo sites for an image you need for a brochure design. Suddenly, the office manager drops a strange card on your desk. You open the mysterious card to find what looks like a poem, but there's something different about it. It's directing you to go somewhere, but you don't know where and you don't know why. **Someone is trying to tell you something.** This is a clue.

You spend the next two nights scouring the Internet for information you found in the clue. There's a biblical code that leads you to a French painter who leads you to a gallery opening tomorrow night. This must be it. You head down to the opening, not sure what to look for or what you'll find.

The doorman hands you a note, as if he knows you. The note is written in the same voice as the one you received earlier. It's another clue. You follow this to a painting, which leads you to a suitcase under the stairs. The suitcase contains only a black light and another clue. This leads you to a pub blocks away, each clue getting tougher to crack, but you must know what lies at the end of this. You follow the clues, one after another, meeting strangers in the dark who pass you coded messages and mysterious glances. Is this a masked message for help? Does this journey lead to unclaimed riches? Is this the plot of a movie and you've been thrust into the starring role?

Nope. This is Ravenchase.

Ravenchase Adventures creates and produces custom adventure races through cities and countrysides all over the world. Using riddles, anagrams, puzzles, actors and the far reaches of imagination, Ravenchase creates races that rival cinematic stories like *The Game, National Treasure* and *Indiana Jones.* The biggest difference, though, is that this is in real life and it stars you. You solve the clues, you make the choices and you risk the reward.

With both public and private games, Ravenchase creates adventures for corporate events, tourism, advertising campaigns and more. You've watched *The Amazing Race*, and now you can live it.

What does all this have to do with a team-centric creative process? These aren't scavenger hunts, these are intricate stories that are being woven in and out of real life. In many ways, it rivals the complexity of creating multi-faceted marketing campaigns in time, ideation and process. **This is the creative process on speed**, and Mid-Atlantic Regional Director and Creative Gadgetologist Lisa Duty is the pharmacist on duty (pun absolutely intended). Lisa and partner Chris Dove have been running the show for the past two years while founder Josh Czarda moved to Hawaii to set up shop.

Just how does Lisa and her band of adventure-loving misfits come up with all these amazing races? "We never stop looking," Lisa says. "Like any creative, looking at things in the light of finding usable ideas is something we have ingrained in us. We can't turn it off. *Our goal is to find the extraordinary in the everyday. We look for small bits of details that most people look at every day but never really see.* Most of what we use we take back and write to, but some things simply write themselves, they're so unique."

The process of creating the games is both unique and familiar, as the process mirrors that of a traditional creative agency, but the project isn't an ad campaign or a branding package, it's an adventure. "It's very similar to the process familiar to most creative firms," Lisa reveals. "We have an initial meeting with the client to talk about boundaries, scope and budget. When we have custom games, we obviously have more boundaries, as most clients have specific goals and unique restrictions that we may not have in the public games we create ourselves. Like a traditional agency environment, we can do some really cool stuff that will have a massive impact, but if it's not on strategy and not on budget, it does no good. It's very much like a traditional creative agency process.

Also like traditional agencies, our team differs from project to project. Depending on the size of the project, we could have anywhere from two to ten people working on an adventure. Every project has unique characteristics, and we are fortunate enough to have a unique team of characters to match. In all seriousness, we work with some of the most brilliant, inventive and creative minds around. **The project team selection is based on the unique experiences and strengths each person possesses and shares with our group. We rely on their own individual creative processes to work through the challenges, but we have a distinct voice and method that needs to come through the work, so everything is measured against that."**

While the writing of the clues and the assembly of the game plan can be done individually, the overall concept of the story and the ideation of possible clues and journeys are done together. "Whether it's near home or abroad," Lisa explains, "When we start a new game, we assign a project lead and begin to engage in an overview of the location. We walk around and look at as much as we can, but we're not looking at it like tourists. We're looking at it with a much more focused purpose. We draw on the experiences we have creating other games, and we start naturally looking for things we can use in the clues.

"We take a ton of digital pictures as we research the area, and while we're doing that, we start to come up with ideas. We start to get a picture for what we can do and that starts to lead our brainstorming. As we're gathering pieces, we're talking and sharing ideas. Often, we'll split up to cover more ground, and we'll end up visiting the same places throughout the day, but we'll see it in a different way. That new perspective often leads to great ideas.

"Once we have done our research and we have a large amount of possibilities, we start in with a lot of word play or image play. What helps in this process is there's really no way to be wrong, just different ways to make the idea or clue stronger. Ultimately, it's the project lead's responsibility to choose what works and what doesn't, so they keep us on track as to the strategy of the project."

The challenge Lisa faces, just like anyone who leads a team of free-thinkers and idea-generators, is how to take the individual creative processes and bring them all together into one cohesive unit.

"I have seen two very distinct styles in our team's individual approaches to creating the games," Lisa discusses. "One is a more right-brained style, where they typically start with what happens at the end of the game, what is the goal, where are they being led, then work backwards from there. Others are a bit more left-brained in their approach—they take the individual parts, these random pieces, and form them together to work for the goal. We tend to put similar styles together, where they can really work well together because they think alike, then when they complete the plan and have completed all the pieces, we review it and provide them another stylistic approach in the review that often exposes things they may not have considered. While it may seem to be a linear process, in that the game takes you from one place to the next, it's more like developing an intricate story. The course of the story and all the parts along the way have to be known before you can begin. It's like those string mazes, where you have a start and an end, but the middle is a spaghetti-looking labyrinth. It's not a straight line start to finish, so the review process is important to make sure it's as solid a direction as possible.

"It gets more complicated as you bring in the real-life aspects to what we create. For instance, if a client in Washington, DC, wants to do something along the National Mall, we may have to look at something like the protest schedule to see what's going on, or find out if there are foreign dignitaries or celebrities in town who may have an impact on the locations we'd like to use. We have to balance the unusual things we'd like people to see while on the adventure, with places that we should avoid during certain times because real circumstances would impede the adventure. The unscripted nature of real life weaving its way into the game adds a level of adventure that makes the game more exciting and authentic, but it also adds an unexpected element to consider while we create the games. Some clients ask us or expect the game to be like a

movie, but movies are scripted and cut to work perfectly. We don't get that luxury. *We weave fantasy into real life, and with that comes certain obstacles that we can only partly control.* It all adds to the authenticity of the game. It's better than a movie script. It's life, it's real and it gives you the opportunity to do more than watch somebody else do it. You get to do it!"

Now that you have an idea of what Ravenchase is, consider the process Ravenchase employs. **If we, as creatives, took the steps they take as part of our creative process, how much more would we learn to see in our everyday lives?** Out of necessity, they take the time to go where their audience will be, to interact with the very things their audience will interact with. They explore and see, ideate and test. Their thorough and committed process is an example of what can be accomplished if we'd look for the extraordinary behind the ordinary.

An Exercise from Ravenchase

Say the word "code" and ask your team what comes to mind. They may say:

Website
Code of ethics
Color-coded
Code violation
Code orange alert
Passcode

The fact is, we're surrounded by codes.

We hop in the car to drive to work. The roadway signs contain symbols and are certain colors. They are codes. Before getting to work, we stop for coffee and use a debit card. We're asked to put in our PIN code. We get to work, fire up the computer and start reading e-mail. The alphabet we read is a code. Later, we head out for lunch and since we're in a hurry and thinking about the many projects we have on our plate, we don't notice that we are driving 45 in a 25-mph zone. But the nice officer on the motorcycle was kind enough to notice us. So he writes a traffic ticket because we have violated a traffic code.

We return to work, where we are preparing a stellar campaign to pitch to the client. It perfectly communicates the client's message so that everyone will want that new what's-it she's selling. We have created a new code for the client.

After work, we stop by our tax preparer's office. Hopefully he is familiar with the latest tax code so that we get that nice refund we're expecting. We continue on our way home and we remember that we wanted to do something nice for our spouse, so we stop by the florist to buy roses. We remember that the number of roses we buy and their colors have certain meanings. How many roses and what color should we buy?

Finally, we arrive home to find our teenager feverishly texting a friend even though we told her to do her homework first. As we take away the phone and send her to her books, we glance down look at the strange code she sent, "g2g bbl." We realize that chatspeak is a code we have trouble understanding.

After dinner, we put on our sneakers to go for a walk and pass by an old cemetery. The ornamentation on an old headstone contains a code that hints at the life of the person buried there and his family's hopes for his afterlife.

Yes, my friends, in life and in death, we are surrounded by codes.

Here's a very flexible exercise. If your team is small, you can do this together. If it's more than four people, break up into smaller teams. You can decide if you want individuals or small groups to make the final contributions to the Code Book you're going to create.

Exercise: Create a Code Book

Your team is going to make a book of codes from images of unusual codes found in your town. (In reality, you can create whatever end product you like, such as a movie. I personally find the printed page more appealing than any other medium.)

Plan:

Decide the dimensions of the book, what substrate to use, how it will be printed, how it will be bound, how many submissions each person or group should contribute, etc. Decide if individuals will have additional assignments, such as cover creation, table of contents, deadline, etc.

Brainstorm:

As a group, define what a code is. Google it and look at all of the possibilities. Discuss codes that the team encounters throughout the day and throughout life.

Research:

Go on a field trip in search of the most unusual codes in your town. You can divide the town into sections—north, south, east, west—or whatever make sense for your locale. You don't have to divide the town, but it's a nice option if you think that folks will gravitate to the same places. If you divided your team into smaller groups, let the groups pick a section or sections to visit.

Each individual or group (depending upon how your team has divided) should take a digital camera.

Find and photograph the most unusual codes you encounter. Take your photos from interesting angles and perspectives. Good places to look are museums, cemeteries, roads, buildings, libraries, parks and monuments. Remember that you are looking for the most unusual code you can find, or perhaps something that folks don't normally think of as a code. It could be something that you regularly pass but have not really noticed. The examples of places listed above are just that, but don't feel you have to limit your group to these places.

Debrief:

Individuals or groups should pick their favorite finds and print them out for group discussion. The images could also be collected and placed in a slide show, which can be projected for discussion purposes. Folks should be prepared to explain something about the code. If they are unsure of the code but thought it was strange or unusual, other individuals from the team may be able to add to the information.

Create:

Prepare the submissions, which should include the images plus a short write-up for each one. The write-up could go on accompanying page from the spread. The write-up needs to include a photo credit, where the image was taken and what the code means, if known. If the code is a mystery, that's OK. The write-up could encourage the reader to help solve the mystery.

Produce:

Make a copy of the Code Book for each team member. Make extra copies as coffee-table books for your company or for others with whom you wish to share your creativity.

281

Index

2 Person Exercises

More Index

Some More Index

3 Person Exercises

...And Even More Index

4 Person Exercises

Surprise! More Index!

I Bet You Can't Guess What This Page Contains

Interviews

Contributors

Ann Willoughby, Willoughby Design Group, www.willoughbydesign.com

Chris Duh, Kaleidoscope, www.hallmarkkaleidoscope.com

Clint Runge, Archrival, www.archrival.com

Dave Gouveia and Chris Elkerton, 3 Dogz Creative, www.3dogz.com

Debbie Millman, Sterling Brands, www.sterlingbrands.com

Eric Chimenti, Chapman University, www.rubricator.net

Jenn and Ken Visocky O'Grady, Enspace, www.enspacedesign.com

John January, Sullivan, Higdon and Sink, www.wehatesheep.com

Justin Ahrens, Rule29, www.rule29.com

Lisa Duty, Ravenchase Adventures, www.ravenchase.com

Sam Harrison, www.zingzone.com

The HOW Forum, forum.howdesign.com

More Great Titles from HOW Books!

Caffeine for the Creative Mind
250 Exercises to Wake Up Your Brain

Packed with 15-minute simple and conceptual exercises, this guide will have readers reaching for markers, pencils, digital cameras, and more in order to develop a working and productive creative mindset.
ISBN: 1-58180-867-4, paperback, 360 p., #Z0164

The Web Designer's Idea Book

The Web Designer's Idea Book includes more than 700 websites arranged thematically so you can find inspiration of layout, color, style and more. It's a must-have for starting any new web projects.
ISBN: 978-1-60061-064-6, paperback, 250 p, #Z1756

Creative Sparks

This playful collection of rock-solid advice, thought-provoking concepts, suggestions and exercises is sure to stimulate the creative, innovative thinking that designers need to do their jobs well. It will encourage readers to find inspiration in the world around them, spark new ideas and act as a guide to each designer's creative path.
ISBN: 978-1-58180-438-6, hardcover, 312 p, #32635

These and other great HOW Books titles are available at your local bookstore, from online suppliers and at
www.howbookstore.com

www.howdesign.com

HOW
BOOKS